# *Vito's*
## Journey II

# *Vito's*
# Journey II

## *The Forks in the Path of Life*

VITO A. LEPORE

VITO'S JOURNEY II
THE FORKS IN THE PATH OF LIFE

iUniverse books may be ordered through booksellers or by contacting:

iUniverse
1663 Liberty Drive
Bloomington, IN 47403
www.iuniverse.com
1-800-Authors (1-800-288-4677)

Because of the dynamic nature of the Internet, any web addresses or links contained in this book may have changed since publication and may no longer be valid. The views expressed in this work are solely those of the author and do not necessarily reflect the views of the publisher, and the publisher hereby disclaims any responsibility for them.

Any people depicted in stock imagery provided by Thinkstock are models, and such images are being used for illustrative purposes only.
Certain stock imagery © Thinkstock.

ISBN: 978-1-4917-5204-3 (sc)
ISBN: 978-1-4917-5203-6 (e)

Library of Congress Control Number: 2014919175

Printed in the United States of America.

iUniverse rev. date: 11/17/2014

# DEDICATION

## TO MY BROTHERS,
## MICHELINO AND MIKEY

Michelino - 1934

Mikey - 1944

The first memories of my life are of the days spent with my brother, affectionately called Michelino. Born on 11/17/1932, he was over two years younger than me. I really only remember the last year of his life, for he died on 3/31/1935, just about two years and four months old.

In that last year, the age difference meant nothing. We were best buddies, and I was always amazed at how bright he was. When my grandfather would knock on the bottom of the kitchen table, and say there was someone at the door, I would jump out of my chair to go answer. Michelino instead laughed, and said, "Nonno, you're doing that yourself." How come I didn't know that, even when it was done more than once? Yeah, yeah, I eventually caught on.

Once, I teased him too much, and he bit me between my shoulder blades (a feat in itself). I went complaining to my mother, who said, "If he did that to you, then you must have deserved it." I knew she was right.

He caught my cold, which developed into pneumonia, and we lost him in a few months. However, even when he was very sick and wasting away, he was a treasure. I remember a day, and the picture is still vivid in my mind. I was sitting on the floor playing with toys, keeping him company while he sat in the high chair, with my mother trying to get him to eat something. He had lost weight, and didn't have the strength to stand on his own, and he saw that we were not very happy. In a very earnest voice, he said, "Mamma, don't worry. If I die, you'll have another Michele". I wasn't even five, but I was flabbergasted that he would say such a thing. My mother and I looked at each other, and we never forgot that moment.

I've had survivor's guilt my whole life. Fortunately, my mother made Michelino's prophecy come true, and Mikey was born on 09/23/1938. I was almost eight years old, and in my fantasy world, I've always believed that Michelino had found a way to come back and fulfill what he had started.

Mike has exceeded all those fantasies.

Thank you

# TABLE OF CONTENTS

# PREFACE

"Vito's Journey II" picks up where "Vito's Journey" left off, but with a different focus. The first book is primarily an introduction of family members, and stories of a boy's transition from Italy to America. Here, we will start from the first step out into an adult world, and go through the stages that come with it.

Boyhood or adulthood, there is one constant; those forks in the path of life. Decisions are made, sometimes on a daily basis, which affect that life. There is no doubt that but for a number of decisions, some not mine, my first twenty years could have gone in a totally different direction. The same is true for my adulthood.

I think that's true for everyone. That being the case, there is no such thing as a "last chance", regardless of age.

I hope the reader is entertained by my roller-coaster life, and acts on the positive message.

Happy trails,

Vito

# 1950 – 1959

**Author's note:** *This is the most important period of my life. Decisions were made that affected the coming years, and my character became defined. In preparing to write about it, I've debated with myself about how detailed I should be, especially about my "sexual awakening". I've decided to tell the story without necessarily getting into the nitty-gritty details, unless it serves a purpose. We'll see how it comes out. If the reader has reservations about reading such material, I would advise to skip ahead to 1954, and the sub-title "Life after the Military".*

Having graduated from Cardinal Hayes High School in June, I was scheduled to start classes at NYU in the fall. However, I thought I had the ability to be a major league baseball player, and I wanted to give that a try first. To finance my dream, I got a job at Cudahy's in the city, working nights loading and unloading boxcars at their warehouse.

My new life started exactly on New Year's Day 1950. That was the day I left home to see if I had a future as a professional baseball player. I had signed up to attend a baseball school and tryout camp in Florida, run by the

1

Washington Senators, at their minor league facility for the Chattanooga Lookouts. My memory is that it was for 6-8 weeks, but I'm not sure. I was nineteen years old.

My father had a hard time coming to terms with my ambition, but agreed to let me try. Uncle Larry knew it was a big moment for me, and wanted to give me a proper sendoff. So, instead of taking the subway to Penn Station, he called for a taxi, and they both accompanied me. For me, it was an adventure, and I couldn't wait to get started. I had been away before, when I had gone to Syracuse, but that was going from family to family. This was to be all by myself. I promised my mother I would be careful.

We got to Penn Station, and to the train that would take me to Orlando, Florida. Uncle Larry said they would take the subway back home, and told me to take care of myself. With about fifteen minutes before departure, my father decided that this was the time to talk to me about "the birds and the bees". Not that we had ever come close to ever having had such a discussion before, or maybe because we hadn't had one, or more probably because my mother may have told him to "talk to him".

Anyway, he was clearly uncomfortable, but went ahead anyway. His advice was as memorable as it was short. Holding me by the arm, he said (in his Coratino dialect), "Vitino, ti raccomando, non si shen multu-en p-daerr'." Phonetically, that's about how it sounds. Loosely translated, it means, "Vitino, please don't go rolling around on the floor." Now, you may find it strange, but I knew exactly what he was telling me. Those few words conjure up images of improper behavior. However, I didn't know how to answer, other than to mumble something about not to worry. Fortunately, uncle Larry had overheard, and came to my rescue. Laughing all the while, he took my father by the arm, and guided him away, saying, "Beh, 'gnazio, lai veramente cacato – sha-ma-nin" meaning, "Ignazio, it looks like you've really crapped up the moment – let's go." They left, and I was alone!

It took 23 hours to get to Orlando, from winter to summer, from civilization, as I knew it, to the one seen in the movies. It was a long ride, made longer because I only had a coach seat to sleep in. I walked the length of the train many times, and was fascinated by all the stops, the different kinds of people, the dining car, and conversations with strangers. When asked, I would tell them I was going to try out for the Washington Senators, and noticed that they were impressed. Yes, the life of a major league baseball player was made for me.

During the frequent stops, I stayed very close to the train if I stepped off, for fear that it would leave without me if it saw me wandering away. I was tired but excited when we pulled into Orlando the following day, looking forward to the unknown in a strange land. It didn't take long to notice the first difference. Taking the bus from the train station into town, I saw no one sitting in the back, and I knew that was because it was reserved for colored people. Mr. Fields, the janitor in Richie's building on 243rd Street, had told me about how different it was for him when he went to visit his family down south. So, on behalf of Mr. Fields, I sat in the back of the bus! I figured somebody would say something, and I'd get a chance to say something about the American way. Nothing! They didn't even know I was there!

After getting into town, and checking into a hotel (I wasn't scheduled to report to camp until the next morning), I went walking around Orlando, which wasn't all that big. Disney hadn't even thought about it at that time. As I said, the Jim Crow laws were unfair, and I was glad I was white. I didn't see any colored people stepping off the sidewalk to let white people pass (as Mr. Fields had said), but I didn't see any of them in any of the stores or restaurants that I entered. I was shocked to see separate water fountains, a few feet from each other, marked "white" and "colored". I was even more shocked that they observed the signs, and no one protested.

I had left freezing weather in New York, and found summertime. Still, as I walked around in my shirtsleeves that evening, a woman in front of me stopped to look at a sidewalk thermometer. Turning to her husband, she said, "I knew I should have taken my fur coat. It's 70 degrees!" Was she kidding? I also ate at a place that had a dinner special. For $1.50, I got a steak that hung off the ends of a big oval platter, plus potatoes and soda and coffee, and a piece of apple pie! What a deal! I also went to a bar that had live music. Like another world! I didn't recognize any of the music. The jukebox didn't have one band that I recognized. Actually, they had no bands at all. Everything was hillbilly music (that was before they decided to call it country western). I would have paid double to hear Harry James, Benny Goodman, or any of the big bands. All I got was pling-plinging guitars and stories about drunks, and jail, and dying for all kinds of reasons.

The next morning I took the bus to Winter Garden, and reported to the ballpark. Actually, it had four ball fields, and a few bungalows, which contained the office, eating facilities, and sleeping quarters. The whole complex was surrounded by an orange, tangerine, and grapefruit grove. The place made Syracuse look like Manhattan.

About sixty would-be major leaguers showed up, and the instructors were major league ballplayers. The only one I remember was "Bobo" Newsome, who had pitched for the Washington Senators, and had a reputation for clowning around. He was a funny guy.

For me, it was Heaven, but not right away. Up early in the morning; breakfast by 8:00 AM, and on the fields by nine. The first week was reviewing basics: running the bases, stealing, soft throwing, doing wind sprints, analyzing batting stances, etc. In the second week, we actually began to swing the bat, and play in the field. The third week we actually began to have some competitive games. It was a great time, and I figured this was going to be my life. I had never had a similar experience. Surrounded by guys about my age who were from all over the country, I learned about other ways of life. Not surprisingly, my best buddies were Jesse James and "The Sheriff". I don't remember their real names. The nights were a hoot. The dormitory was a row of double-decked bunks, and as soon as it was "lights out", it was the beginning of fun time. In the dark, someone would tell a joke, then someone else would try to top it. Soon, it was non-stop. For me, the most entertaining part was listening to all the different accents, and the humor that reflected the area that the speaker came from. Almost all the kids were "country" boys, and like me, this was their first experience away from home. Not all the jokes were good, and when one was not received well, the one who had told it would be bombarded with slices of tangerines stored for the occasion. My own valise was full of ammunition. Of course, since it was dark, we could only guess at where our target was, and many innocent people got "tangerined". The night supervisor would come and quiet us down, but it didn't last long.

The town of Winter Garden was real country. It consisted of one main street, with a railroad track running down its length. There was a small shed where the lone police officer would stay, if he wasn't driving around in the patrol car. There was one movie house, which opened for one show nightly. All the fruit stores left their products outside on the sidewalk for the night. Not much to do. There was a bar, and it was fun listening to the major league instructors' talk about life in the big time, having a beer, and playing shuffleboard, but I could only take so much of that. So one night, Jesse, the Sheriff, and I decided to take a walk outside of town. That's when we found out that the ballplayers were not liked there. As we were walking along a dark road, a couple of cars passed and threw oranges at us, but only Jesse got hit. When they turned to make another pass, we started running, and were lucky to spot a coffee shop. Unfortunately, the owner didn't want any trouble, and wouldn't let us in. The cars emptied, and we found ourselves surrounded by 10-15 kids our age, who started cursing at us, and who were working themselves up to do something more serious. Being a city boy, and having spent a lot of time in the movies, I knew the best way to handle it was to take on the ringleader, and I did a very stupid thing. I went right up to the biggest loudmouth, and said, "You talk like Jimmy Cagney. I wonder if you can fight like him". Well, it had the desired effect. All the other guys quieted down, and looked to see what he was going to do. Me? My legs started to shake, and I realized I was going to get it good. The guy was bigger than me, looked a lot stronger, and my fighting experience was next-to-nothing. The only thing holding him back was that he was trying to figure out if I really had anything besides a big mouth.

Fortunately, the coffee shop owner had called the cop, and he came driving up just in time. He knew all the kids, and told them to leave us alone, but he wouldn't give us a ride back to town. The guys got in their cars and left, as did the cop, and we knew we were going to get it before we got back to town. We heard some singing, and traced it to a recreation center behind a church. Needing a place to hide, we went in, and were welcomed by the townspeople, who had gathered for a church social. We were given milk and cookies, and introduced to their daughters, who were our age. Apparently, they liked us for the same reason that the guys hated us. We were competition, and while the local guys were stuck there, the ballplayers passing through represented a possible escape and a better life for the girls. We sang some hymns, and got religion for a couple of hours. We made it back to camp without incident, and didn't stray out of town after that, not even for the girls.

The ball playing was great, and I thought I was doing pretty well. "Bobo" was my coach, and I thought I had impressed him. I was batting over .300, and I was pretty proud of myself, except for one instance. During one game, the other coach, who also was a major league pitcher, decided to get some work in, and came in to pitch. Unfortunately, I happened to be the batter. It was pretty clear that he was just loosening up, but I had never seen such a fastball. It was past me before I knew it. I never got a chance to lift the bat off my shoulder. Fortunately, he missed the plate, and walked me. I strutted to first base, giving the impression that he had been afraid to pitch to me, but inside I was wondering if I would ever be able to hit that kind of pitching.

In the last two weeks of camp, the instructors had made their decisions, and some guys were being offered contracts to play minor league ball. They would do this by calling the player's name on the loudspeaker, and told to come to the office. Of course, while we were playing, we all had one ear listening for such a call. Of course, I knew I was better than every guy that was called, and wondered when they would get around to me. So, I wasn't surprised to hear, "Lepore, to the office". As I jogged towards the office, past the envious looks of my teammates, I started debating what kind of offer would be made, and if I should accept it or try to negotiate a better deal. I wondered how long it would take for me to get to play in the major leagues, and what team I would wind up with. When I walked into the office, I was trying so very hard not to grin, because I wanted to be very professional about this. I went to the desk and asked, "You wanted to see me?" With barely a glance up, I was told, "Yeah. You didn't make your bed this morning. Go do it now".

As I headed for the bunkhouse, I remembered the story my mother used to tell, about the woman bringing the eggs to market, who started daydreaming. She figured that she would save some of the eggs, and hatch them to make more chickens. Then she would have more eggs, and she would hatch more chickens, until she would have so many that the townsfolk would respect her, and when they would pass her on the street, they would bow and say, "Buon giorno, signora maestra". She bowed as she imagined this, forgetting that she was carrying the eggs in a basket, balanced on her head. Of course, all the eggs splattered, along with her dreams. The American version tells us not to count our chickens before they're hatched. Either way, I was deflated, and I would have preferred to have gone right home, rather than go back out on the field to tell my buddies "what I had been offered".

When it became clear that I wasn't going to be called, I went to see "Bobo" Newsome to find out why. He told me that I had average speed and arm, and that my fielding needed improvement. I needed to know what to do with the ball before it got to me. My hitting was OK, but he advised I needed a year of semi-pro ball experience. Camp ended, and we said our goodbyes, promising to visit each other, but outside of an isolated letter, it all became just a memory. I would have stayed in Florida longer, but jobs only paid 40 cents an hour, and hard to find.

*     *     *

### The Big Decision –

Back home, it was still cold, and I told my Florida adventure to anyone who wanted to hear it. I always felt special before, but now I knew it for sure. I had experiences that others didn't have, had graduated from Cardinal Hayes, and was very smart. No, that wasn't what anyone had been telling me. It was just something that I believed. However, I never behaved like a snob. I was a regular guy. My only problem was that I didn't have a steady girlfriend.

I was scheduled to start attending NYU in the fall, and I had a few months on my hands. I figured to get a job, and to check out some of the semi-pro baseball teams in the area for the summer. It seemed that my future was pretty much back on track, when my mother asked me if I would like to go to Italy with her for the summer! WOW! It seems that my parents had agreed to sell their property in Corato, since they weren't getting any income from it. My father always spoke of working all those years, and not even having his own home to show for it. They agreed that my mother should go, so that my father could continue working, and not lose those wages. She would take Mike, because he was too young to leave behind, but I'm not sure of the reason I was invited. Maybe my father couldn't imagine having to look after me; maybe they figured I wouldn't be able to take care of myself; maybe it was just what it appeared, an opportunity to see the family we had left behind in 1940, maybe for the last time.

*****Note: Oct. 15, 2010***** – Mike is reading my writings, and comments that my going to Italy was discussed in my absence. It seems that I had expressed an interest in meeting Italian girls. Also, my father was concerned about my present girlfriend, Vilma Coletti, and her intention to become a nurse. He didn't want her to be coming home to me, after washing other peoples' private parts. How funny is that? That was <u>my</u> concern! Read my article on Vilma. Just goes to show, great minds think alike.

## **Vilma Coletti – Copied from "Vito's Journey"**

Standing in the rear of a movie theatre, we struck up a conversation with a couple of girls, and after the movie, Richie, Roddy, and I walked them home. I couldn't get one of the girls out of my mind, and a few weeks later I got up enough courage to go to her house on 229th Street. It was a three-story building and I didn't know her last name, so I rang all the bells, and stood at the bottom of the stairs asking to speak to Vilma. Eventually she showed up, and had no idea who I was. Obviously, I hadn't made as big an impression on her, but soon remembered, and invited me upstairs. I met the mother, and was further captivated. Vilma was a first-generation American like me, the parents were from Venice, and still spoke Italian to the daughter. The musical tone of the Venetian dialect was intoxicating. In fact, everything about the girl was so positive, I would have proposed marriage on the spot. Of course that couldn't be, but I was sure I had found my life-partner. The fact that I didn't know anything about her didn't matter. I had that feeling. Of course I had had that feeling with Lucy, Mary Rapetti, and others, but this was <u>the real thing!</u>

We went out a couple of times, to a movie or for an ice cream, and it was great, until she told me about what she wanted to do with her life. She wanted to work, and she wanted to become a nurse! My God, this was not acceptable! I figured I should be the center of her universe, with no need for her to work. I would provide, although I didn't have a clue about how. The worst part though, was her being a <u>nurse</u>! To me, that meant that she would see and tend to naked men other than myself! Totally out of the question! I tried to talk her out of it, but she was committed. So, our relationship cooled, but I've always thought I made more out of it than she did. I wrote to her when I was in Italy, and even double-dated with Mario when I came back, but it was not to be.

She did become a nurse, and shortly before I was to be married, I ran into her. She and another nurse were waiting for a bus after work at a hospital in Mt. Vernon, when I passed in my car. I gave them a ride home, and Vilma told her friend what a great catch I would be for some girl. I can't deny I derived a little bit of pleasure from informing them that I had already been snagged, and that I had a business in Italy, where we would be going to after getting married. I've always felt a little bad about the way I said that, but she's the one who brought up the subject. Besides, I still think I cared more for her than she did for me.

Vilma will always have a special place in my heart. She was my first serious girlfriend. By a strange coincidence that I found out about many many years later, her cousin Mary married my cousin Vito. I was told that she had married, her husband owned a restaurant, and had children. Unfortunately, her husband had died, and she was living somewhere in Yonkers.

*   *   *

Whatever the reason, it was obviously a major decision for me. I really didn't know what to do. Going to Italy was very attractive, but I would be giving up a year's experience in semi-pro ball, not earning any money, and maybe missing out starting at NYU. I had already delayed a year, and I didn't want to lose any more time. What to do? What to do? I didn't have a whole lot of people to get advice from. Uncle Larry told me I should do what I felt I should do. That didn't help, because I wanted to do both at the same time. I asked my buddies, and their consensus was I would be crazy if I didn't go to Italy. That didn't help, because, after all, what the hell did they know?

So it was that I got my best advice from a traditional philosopher. No, not my barber, but my bartender! Over a beer at Barney's, I presented my dilemma to Frank and John, the day and night bartenders. I got them when they were changing shifts, so that I was able to get both of their viewpoints at the same time. After mulling it over, they both agreed I should go to Italy. They both agreed that we can control our decisions, but we can't control opportunities. A chance like this may not happen again, while the worst that could happen would be that my baseball career and college education would be delayed by maybe a year. It made sense to me. None of us could foresee all the other things that could happen, but I was just a kid, and they were, after all, bartenders.

## The Ocean and Land Voyage

So it was that in March or April of 1950 we "sailed" to Europe on the "Queen Elizabeth". In those days, it was cheaper to go by boat than by airplane, I think. Maybe it was because we traveled in tourist class, which was below 1st class and cabin class. Actually, the cabins were at the bottom of the ship, probably on the same level as the engine room. Everyone came to see us off, and it felt like the beginning of another great adventure. Certainly, I remembered my first crossing, so I felt like a veteran. What a life! Being served breakfast, lunch, and dinner; movies and games all day; above us in 1st class were the "rich" people, and the ship's newspaper told us of some of them. My brother remembers that Joan Crawford was on board. I remember Irene Dunn. Anyway, they could have been in another world, for all that we saw of them. Not that we didn't try! I would take Mike with me to explore the ship. Sneaking out of tourist class, we would go up to cabin, and briefly up to 1st class. I wasn't comfortable up there. The people looked different, and I felt like I had "tourist class" stamped on my forehead. I was more at home in cabin class. There, they had a regular movie theatre. In tourist, they would pull down a screen in the dining room, and it was much smaller. The help wasn't as elegant, but I felt privileged to be living this life. My mother stayed put while Mike and I were left to our own devices. She may have suffered some seasickness, because Mike and I had some dinners without her. You would think that I should know something like that for sure, and you'd be right!

Mike did get seasick, and I had a brainstorm to cure it. The ocean was really kicking up, and the ship was rocking. Few people were out on deck, and even less showed up for dinner. I loved it, but Mike got seasick. I figured the best place to be would be in the water! The ship had two big indoor swimming pools. Mike and I were the only ones in the pool, but I was right. While the water was sloshing back and forth, even out of the pool, and the ship was rocking and rolling, we were floating in the center of the pool. I thought I was brilliant. Unfortunately, we couldn't stay there all day, and Mike felt ill outside the pool, although he never threw up. He hung in and hung out with me all day.

After about five days, we docked in Le Havre, France. For the first couple of hours off the ship, I still had my "sea legs", and it felt as if I was still walking on a rolling deck. We took a train to Milan, with a changeover in Paris. I don't recall any French friends or acquaintances, so this was my first exposure to that nationality. Well, I had seen it in the movies, and there was Charles Boyer, and I thought that they would be just like Italians, except that they spoke French. In truth, we weren't there very long, and my opinion was gotten from four representatives of that country: a baggage handler, a waiter, a taxi driver, and a ticket agent. In baseball terms, they went 0 for 4, with four strikeouts!

As I said, we had a stopover in Paris for a few hours. After getting off the train, my mother thought it would be a good idea to make use of the time and take a quick look around the city. We decided to check the baggage at the station until we returned, so I called out to the man wheeling our luggage to stop, so that we could find out where to check the baggage. Unfortunately, he didn't hear me. I called out louder, in English and in Italian, but the man kept walking. Only when I ran past him, turned and stopped in front of him, raised my arm, and said "Halt", did I get any response. He gave me a puzzled expression; as if he didn't have any idea as to what I was talking about. We found it strange behavior.

After checking the baggage, we crossed the street from the station, and went into a restaurant. The menus were in French, and the waiter knew as much English or Italian as the baggage handler. We chose what we hoped would be a pasta dish, and it turned out OK, with no thanks to the waiter.

Back on the street, we figured we had enough time to visit the Eiffel Tower. We hailed a taxi, got in, told the driver to go to the Eiffel Tower, and got a response of "pardon?" Repeated requests got no better results. Only when I started accompanying the request with hand motions denoting a tall structure did the light go on. "Ahhhh, la Torr 'Eiffel?" Only when I repeated "La Torr 'Eiffel" did he understand. Once again, we found it strange that these people didn't understand the most rudimentary words unless they were spoken in French.

We got to the Eiffel Tower, and even climbed it a little ways, until we realized that we had left our portable radio back at the restaurant. We figured we had lost it, but decided to have a look anyway. Once again, we hailed a taxi, but didn't ask to go to the railroad station in English. Instead, it was a French-accented "Garden Lion" (I'm sure that's not the correct spelling). I even rolled my "r" and added a French nasal accent. No problem! We got to the station in no time, and returned to the restaurant. Our friendly waiter was still there, but didn't understand a word of what we were saying. I decided to look for myself, and wonder of wonders, the radio was just where I had left it; on the floor behind my chair, against the wall. I waived it to my waiter as we left the restaurant. At the door, I took another look back, and I saw our waiter talking animatedly to another waiter. From the hand and arm motions I interpreted that he was very angry with himself for having missed out on getting himself a radio. Nice fellow.

Back at the station, we had to get tickets to Milan. I approached the ticket agent, sitting behind a cutout glass window, and asked for the time the next train to Milan left. This person also didn't understand what I was asking, and I found it infuriating. It was so infuriating, that, as I kept repeating myself, I didn't realize that I was forcing myself through that little glass opening, until I was nose-to-nose with the agent behind his desk. My mother and Mike found it very funny, and kidded me about it for a long time. They said all they could see was my rear end sticking out of the ticket agent's window.

We were very happy to be leaving Paris, and I have never had the urge to go back. Especially when the next morning, after crossing into Italy, the Italian customs agent on the train visited every compartment with a big smile and a "Benvenuti in Italia … (Welcome to Italy)". He also said it in French and German. What a difference! If I weren't already Italian, I would have converted on the spot.

My mother took advantage of our stopover in Milan to visit her cousins (on her mother's side). I was impressed by a commendation and medal that they had hanging on the wall. It told of the heroic death of their son in World War II. A hand grenade had been thrown into the trench where his group was, and he had thrown himself on top of it, saving the lives of his comrades. Mike remembers their names, and that they were jewelers. He was very impressed by their shop that we visited. I only remember they were very nice people, and showed us around, including the "Duomo". It's a very large covered shopping mall, and impressive.

The next day they took us to the railway station, and I may already have told this story. If so, I'll edit it, but it's worth retelling.

While my mother and her cousins went to buy the tickets, I waited with the luggage, near the entrance of the gigantic station. After a while, the cousin signaled to me. Palm outward, he raised his arm, and then forward and down (like a swimming stroke). It looked like he was telling me to back up. I didn't know why, but I took the luggage, and backed up a few feet. He then repeated the motion a second time, with more emphasis. I figured I hadn't moved back far enough, so I took the luggage and moved back even more. He then started repeating the motion over and over, in a very excited manner. The only thing I could figure was that they were buying a child's ticket for me, and didn't want the agent to see me. So, I turned and ran out of the station, leaving the luggage behind.

I waited outside in the large piazza until they caught up to me. With concerned and puzzled looks, they wanted to know what was the matter with me? When I explained, they found it hilarious, and couldn't stop laughing, including my mother. It seems that in Italy, that's a signal to come closer. I explained that in America, the signal would be with the palm facing in, and the motion would be an upward one, clearly telling someone to come closer. They weren't convinced, and enjoyed themselves immensely at my expense.

Continuing down, we stopped off in Rome for some sightseeing. What an impressive city. While Milan struck me as an Italian version of New York, Rome was clearly historic, and in a class by itself. Where we measure things by generations, they measure by centuries. The glory years of the Roman Empire were over 1500 years before the discovery of America. Everywhere you looked, you would be struck by the contrast between ancient and modern. I was very impressed.

Unfortunately, we also had a Roman episode. My mother decided to take advantage of being in Rome, and got tickets to the famed opera house, to see "Don Carlos". We had great seats, about the sixth row orchestra. I had never attended an opera, and I couldn't make the mental adjustment that the voice determined the character. I was a movie guy. For example, I couldn't see why the guy would leave a perfectly beautiful girl, to lust after such a fat horse. The lyrics left a lot to be desired. They carried on and on, always saying the same thing, and they took such a long time to die after being mortally wounded. I kept asking my mother to explain, but she kept shushing me.

The straw that broke the camel's back came in the final act, when the heroine (the fat horse) did her highlight solo. Her lover had been killed, and she was expressing her grief. This was the high point of the opera. However, what I saw was a very fat woman, standing on the edge of the stage directly in front of me, making high-pitched sounds that sounded like a chicken. Of course, flapping her arms up and down in her grief only accentuated the image. I started to giggle, and my mother poked me, telling me to behave myself. I shared my vision with her, asking if it didn't look like the woman was going to lay an egg at any moment. After a few moments, she also started to giggle. People starting shushing us, but that only made it worse. So, in the middle of the drama, we had to get up and leave, stepping on many toes on the way out of our row. We went to other operas, and I've developed a liking for some of them, but that first experience was memorable.

Continuing our train journey, we met a couple of memorable Italians. I should mention that European trains are not like the American ones, and you've probably seen them in the movies. First off, like the ship, there is a first class, and a tourist class. Here, we traveled first class. It was comprised of compartments holding six passengers, with a door for privacy. Outside the compartment was a walkway, where a passenger could stretch and mingle with other passengers. In our compartment, we happened to draw two young Italians, and a young American girl who was about my age. The girl was visiting family in Potenza, and didn't speak Italian. The Italians didn't speak English, but developed an instant desire to learn the language. One of them, Alberto DeConcettis, was especially funny. He wanted to know how he could ask people to let him through in the corridor outside, wanting to impersonate being an American. We told him to say, "Please let me through", but he couldn't get it quite right. So, he would go up and down the aisle saying "With the through" over and over. All of this and more, in an obvious effort to impress the girl, who had the three of us guys in the palm of her hand. This was very entertaining for my mother and Mike, and we laughingly recalled the trip many times.

## The Arrival

Eventually, we got to Corato, but not without incident. There was no express stop at Corato, so we got off at Trani, the next town over. It was nighttime when we arrived, and zio Amerigo and zio Gennaro were at the station to meet us. We hadn't seen each other for over ten years, and there was much embracing and tears as we got off the train. So much so, that we forgot to take the luggage off the train. I remembered that when I saw the train pulling out of the station, and I alerted everybody. Later, my uncles were impressed at how calm I was as I was telling them that our valises were on the train that was leaving the station. That's not the Italian way! You're supposed to get all excited, jump up and down, with a lot of arm waving (like the opera singer). That's the way things get done in Italy, which is exactly what my uncles did. They then proceeded to inform the stationmaster, who also started to behave in the same manner, but for a different reason. He couldn't understand how anyone could be so stupid as to get off the train without their luggage. He calmed down when told that we were Americans. "Sono Americani" was an expression that I got to hear frequently. It generally followed some gaffe of behavior, like implying that we were mentally deficient. Anyhow, the stationmaster called ahead, and had the luggage removed at the next station. We drove there, and eventually got to Corato close to midnight. My grandfather and zia Adalgisa (zio Amerigo's wife) were waiting up for us, and we had another round of embracing.

As soon as we walked inside the door of the apartment, the handle of the valise broke, and I found it very funny. I'm sure they must have thought I was rather strange, until I explained the reason. When we left New York, The handle had broken by the time we had gotten to our cabin. We had called the room steward, and asked to see if he could fix it. He proceeded to tie it with some rope, and it didn't look like a good job. He assured us, "Don't worry. This will last until you get where you want to go". Talk about being prophetic!

Clockwise from top: With my grandfather; Anna Vernice, wife of my mother's brother Gennaro, with infant Luciano. My mother and I were the Baptismal Godparents; Uncle Gennaro's villino. He had five boys; Vito and Isa Tedeschi, orphaned children of my mother's sister Esterina; Uncle Amerigo, aunt Adalgisa, and Michele; Michele on my scooter; Uncle Amerigo.

It was very exciting for me to be back in Corato, to see my grandfather and uncle Amerigo again. He hadn't changed a bit, except to be older and married, with a little son named Michele. He saw humor in everything, and time spent with him was as enjoyable as it had been years ago. The fact that his income barely made it possible to put food on the table didn't take away from his demeanor. Even his wife, who as a schoolteacher was more prim and proper, couldn't help but be amused by his antics. Occasionally, she would scold him when she felt he had gone too far, and he would behave like a scolded child, which was even funnier.

One of those incidents happened at the dinner table, the first day we were there. I had to go to the bathroom, and asked where it was. I knew there was no plumbing, but I didn't know where the portable toilet was. It turned out it was right in the kitchen, stored under the furnace. My uncle pulled it out, and so as to give me privacy, everyone got up from the table and went into the next room. Before leaving, my uncle turned to me, and in a serious tone, asked me to stir the gravy pot while I was sitting there. He was joking, of course, and we all laughed, but aunt Adalgisa just shook her head, and reprimanded him, "Amerigooo"! He gave a sheepish grin, raised his eyebrows, and puckered his lips to the side, just like when I was little. I loved my uncle!

Everybody knew him, and everybody liked him. We couldn't go anywhere without someone calling out to him, and they couldn't call his name without smiling. I was with him when he went shopping to the grocery store for that evening's meal. The storeowner delicately tried to tell my uncle that his credit was severely extended, and took out the book to show him the total. Unperturbed, and with that smile, my uncle pointed out that the amount was very uneven, and that when the day's shopping would be added, it would make a nice round number, and much easier to remember. The man couldn't help but smile, shake his head, and give my uncle what he wanted. If there were a degree for knowing how to live in poverty, zio Amerigo would have a Doctorate.

He earned a living as a private chauffer to a commercial landowner, who owned a large olive grove, as well as a mill for pressing the olives into olive oil. He would either chauffer the man, or drive the truck full of olives from grove to mill. The relationship was owner-driver, but very friendly. My uncle was Don Vincenzo's buddy; he participated in his boss's business dealings, and they regularly drank espresso and ate together. On his days off, he could use the car if he needed it. Like everyone else, Don Vincenzo Bombino enjoyed my uncle's company.

Corato had changed little from when I had left it, except that there were more cars on the road. Actually, I should say more vehicular traffic. In addition to all size cars, there were all sizes of trucks, starting with a three-wheeler, which was nothing more than a covered motorcycle pulling a trailer. There were motor scooters, and even motorized bicycles. Of course, there were still the horse-drawn wagons that the farmers used, and driving required much skill. After six at night, it was almost impossible to drive through towns, because the people were out doing their "passeggiata", and they considered having to move over for a car an intrusion on their private life. A memorable example: I had accompanied my uncle and his boss on business out of town, and we were returning to Corato. To try to make better time, my uncle decided to drive through the adjoining town, instead of going around it. It turned out to be very slow going. The streets were full of people, and they wouldn't move without a dirty look or a comment. One guy didn't move at all. As my uncle kept pressing on the horn, he gave us a look, and bent his knees forward, which was supposed to give us room to pass behind him, but his feet were still in the way. Exasperated, my uncle yelled at him to get out of the way. With a dirty look, and lots of arm waving, he yelled back, "Hey, if I was a tree, wouldn't you have to go around me?" At which point, my uncle released the brake, and headed right for him. Then he moved, still cursing and waving.

My grandmother had died, as well as aunt Esterina, leaving behind two orphans, Vito and Isa Tedeschi. Originally, the children had been divided between the brothers. Since uncle Gennaro already had five boys, he took Isa. However, after a while, it became apparent that she was being used more as a maid, and uncle Amerigo took responsibility of both children, even though uncle Gennaro earned more money as a bookkeeper.

Uncle Amerigo and family lived with my grandfather in his apartment that I remembered from childhood. My grandfather still went to his office every day, even though he hadn't had any business for years. Well, maybe a little thing here and there. Every evening, he would pick something up on the way home, maybe some ricotta or fruit or something for the dinner table, which was his way of showing his independence, and he would not sit at the table until everyone else was seated. Dinner would not start, and no one would sit, until he came home. We were told that he was fitted with a tube that carried his urine to a bag that was fitted inside his pants, but we never saw it. He was very private, and always carried himself with dignity, but was not aloof. I always remember the times spent together when I was little. He would pick me up at home, give me a ride on his bicycle out to the cemetery, where he had some work, and then back home. I liked spending time with him, and he always carried some candies in his jacket pockets for me.

For a few days, they made room for us there, but we had to get our own place. It would have been nice if we could have taken over one of our apartments, but that wasn't going to happen. The only empty space available was on the ground floor, which opened up on a back alley behind the apartment. It had a large room, a kitchen with running water, a hallway, and a toilet. My mother had stored some furniture there, including the bedroom, and we moved in. Of course, word spread immediately that the "Americani" had moved into the neighborhood, and every time we stepped out into the alleyway, there would be indirect looks and whispering. No Welcome Wagon lady came welcome us, but you can be sure they knew a lot about us. As an example, a couple of days after arriving, I took Mike with me to get a "gassosa", which was a homemade lemon-flavored soda. Found someone selling it on a back street. As soon as he saw us, he said, "Oh, you're the Americans that arrived the other night at one in the morning!" I was shocked, and asked how he knew that. He just smiled and said, "We know everything."

He was right! Word had spread quickly, and soon I had people coming up to me and introducing themselves as my former classmates. I honestly didn't remember any of them, but it gave me a group to hang out with. They were almost all going to college, which would put them in the upper class of a farming town like Corato. We would meet, walk the "Stradone", they would practice their English on me, and ask to try one of my American cigarettes. When I didn't offer them a cigarette, one or another would ask to take the last puff on my cigarette butt before I threw it away. After a while, it became irritating, and obvious that I was being used. They had a small town mentality, and I started finding reasons not to be with them. There was one exception. A friend of theirs named Vincenzo, wasn't a college man. His family made a living selling "gassose", and he was very entertaining. He also bummed cigarettes, but thanked me profusely every time, and promised that he would pay them back to me. You have to understand that the Italian cigarettes were terrible, and foreign cigarettes were very expensive. You could buy American cigarettes on the black market, but they weren't the same as the real American cigarettes from America! Anyway, I figured Vincenzo was like the rest, but he really surprised me. One night, my mother, Mike, and I were at a circus that was performing in town, when I heard my name being called. Vincenzo came running up to us, and gave me a pack of Lucky Strikes that he had received in a package from America. He was so obviously proud of himself that he could pay me back as he had promised, that I had to take the cigarettes. It showed me that a college education doesn't necessarily bring a sense of honor with it.

## My boyhood buddy, Felice Fiore

Mike had heard the stories about the friend that I remembered, Felice Fiore, and he went out on his own to find him for me. He asked around, tracked him down, and brought him to the house to surprise me. In the picture, Felice is in the center. Mike was only eleven at the time, with a limited Italian vocabulary, and I was amazed at what he did! Just imagine; a little kid in a foreign town, stopping strangers on the street, and asking about a possible resident until he tracked him down. It was an early sign of his determination when he set his mind to something.

Afterwards, I didn't get to see much of Felice, because he was out of town a lot, also attending the university in Bari. It was just as well, because we really didn't have all that much past to talk about, and our futures were uncertain.

Actually, I did see him again, six years later, when I was running La Lampara. I had been advised that we had a very large dinner party coming, and the guest of honor was a big deal politician that had come down from Rome to check on the local leaders. So, we were on our toes, but not nearly as much as the party-people. When he finally showed up, I couldn't see him, because he was totally surrounded by people who were falling all over themselves ass-kissing him. When I finally caught a glimpse, you can imagine my surprise when I recognized Felice. He was slowly making his way forward, coat over his shoulders, shaking hands and making small talk, with a smug, superior smile on his face. It was an Emperor-like entrance! I immediately pushed my way through the crowd, and we hugged like brothers, to the consternation of all present. Arm in arm, as I accompanied him to his table, I whispered in his ear, "Felice, should I tell these good people the story of when we were kids, and were neighbors in the country villas outside of Corato. Remember, we were taking a crap in the vineyards, and those big bugs attacked you? You got so scared, and ran ass-naked through the fields, back to the villino, yelling for your mother to help you from the attacking bugs? Don't you think your friends will enjoy the story?" The color drained from his face, and he whispered back, "Vito, please! I'm a very serious person now!" I gave him a look back. Then, we couldn't help it, and both thought back to the time I had just mentioned. We started to laugh, went into convulsions, and couldn't stop until tears ran down our eyes. The people around us didn't know how to react. Again, we hugged and parted. It seems that in the intervening years, Felice had become a big shot in the Fascist National Party. They were not known as a "fun" party.

However, my other buddies were not short on conversation, and were curious about everything American, comparing it to Italy. For example, they couldn't conceive the fact that in America, a milkman would deliver milk to the house, and just leave it outside the door. "No one picks it up and walks away with it?" they marveled. They also couldn't grasp the idea of a supermarket, where people actually got their own merchandise, and brought it to a cashier. They said Italians couldn't be trusted to do that, that they would hide stuff under their coats, or leave without paying. They also thought that because I lived in America, I must be acquainted with movie stars, and would ask me if I knew this one or that one. Eventually, they understood. We covered a whole lot of other subjects, but being guys, girls were always being discussed. This led to…

## My first sexual experience –

Talking about girls was not my strong subject, but I tried to sound knowledgeable. They also were at a disadvantage, because although it was 1950, Corato was still in the previous century in that department. You just didn't walk up and talk to a girl without an introduction, and no self-respecting girl would give you the time of day without a chaperone of some kind, without risking her reputation permanently. It was a world of signals, and connections, and conniving, for couples to come together. Of course, there was the exception, where a girl would defy the family, and take off with her true love. However, if they didn't get married, she became a "ruined" woman, but marriage didn't guarantee family acceptance. It had not happened for my grandfather, and the rules had not changed since.

So, we would review the girls as they passed, doing the "passeggiata" on the "Stradone". I was amazed at the amount of personal information they had on each girl, considering how strict the town was. For example, they pointed out a girl that was "loose". When I asked what she had done, I was answered by a nodding smirk, accompanied by a clockwise rotating of an open right hand. This meant she was very, very "loose". Now I was even more curious, because maybe this was possible "action". So, I asked for more details. How disappointing! It seems that the town held occasional dances at the Town Hall (Municipio), as a way for families to have fun, and for young people to meet. Families had their own tables, and a young man would ask permission to dance with the daughter. If he was known, and approved of, he would get that permission, and all eyes would be on them until she was returned to the table. Being a college student was a major plus, so my buddy got the OK to dance with the pretty girl. He proceeded to brag about how, when they were dancing, he maneuvered her to the center of the couples, out of sight of the parents. There, they danced "close". Once again, this was accompanied by a nodding smirk, and a clockwise rotation of the open right hand. I insisted on knowing the details. Did he grab her butt, or any other important part? No. Did she grab his crotch or rub really close? Noooo. She just agreed to dance close, although not touching. Seeing my disappointment, he asked his buddies if it wasn't true. They all agreed, since they had also had gotten to dance with her. To myself, I thought "what a shame". These guys were ruining this girl's reputation. If I hadn't persisted in knowing the details, I would have gone away thinking all of them had slept with her. As I said before, a college education doesn't automatically bring a sense of honor with it, especially in Corato.

For this reason, I was always careful about how I behaved around my newfound friends, and how I answered their questions. I didn't want to come across as just another stupid American. So, when they asked if there were "casinos" in America, I was at a loss. I thought they were talking about a place to gamble. I learned that "Casino'", with the accent on the "o", was what I thought. Without the accent on the "o", it was a bordello. In those days, I knew it as a whorehouse. I told them that I didn't know of any, trying to sound like a man of the world, who had no need to have to pay for those services. They should know! I found out they were legal in Italy, and there was one in almost every town, including Corato.

I turned down their invitation to go with them to the local Casino, but asked about where the best one around was. Being an American, I obviously could afford the best, so they told me it was "Il Villino Delle Rose" in Bari. They gave me directions, but only had second-hand information, because it was expensive.

My mother, Mike, and I had been to Bari a couple of times since arriving. As I said, we had a toilet in the apartment, but no bathtub or shower. My mother would heat up some water, pour it in a basin, and we would sponge bathe. Bari had a public bath, and we would go there periodically. A private room with a bathtub and all the hot water you would want! What a luxury! Then we would make a day of it and go to the movies or to the opera house. I always looked forward to our Bari trips. It was about 30 miles away, and a 45-minute bus ride.

So, once again by myself, I took the bus to Bari, and my great adventure. I had read about these "houses", and seen them in movies, but this was a chance to see it "live". Plus, my only experience was some innocent kissing with nice girls. To say that I was nervous would be an understatement.

I found my way to the street, but I didn't have an exact address. They had told me I couldn't miss it, but I saw no sign above any doorway, or any traffic of people going in and out of any building. "Villino delle Rose" translates into "The Villa of Roses", and I thought that might be a clue, since this was a nice residential neighborhood on the outskirts of the city. The only place that I thought qualified was a Salumeria (grocery store), which was set back from the street, with a patch of bare earth on either side of the walk up to the entrance. I figured that roses were not in season yet, and that the grocery store was a front, with the Casino in the back. Besides, this was the only place that there was any traffic of people, so it had to be it!

I walked in, and it looked like any other Salumeria. People behind the counter, people ordering stuff, and there seemed to be a back room, but nobody was going in or out of there except the clerks. I figured it was just a matter of timing, and I certainly wasn't going to ask if this was a Casino! So, I ordered a sandwich, and started to eat it right there in the store, which no one else was doing. I finished the sandwich, and still hadn't a clue on how to get into the Casino. I figured business must be really slow, seeing as how it was daytime. I needed an excuse to stay in the store, so I ordered another sandwich. Since the first had been a very big sandwich, the clerks marveled at my appetite, but it seemed like they were beginning to look at me funny. By the time I finished my second "panino", it dawned on me that this was really just a Salumeria. Worse yet, it didn't sell sodas, and I had nothing to wash down those two panini! Can you imagine the reaction if I had asked them the directions to the Casino?

So, back out on the street, I looked for the next possibility. There was a three-story building on the corner, and it had a second metal door inside the vestibule from the street entrance. This was different! I pushed the doorbell, not having a clue as to what to say if someone answered. Sure enough, a small window in the door opened, and after a few seconds, closed. The metal door opened, and a kindly looking grandmother smilingly asked, "Si, Signore?" I just wanted to run away, but my legs wouldn't move. They had told me that there would be a person at the door, but this was somebody's grandmother! It couldn't be the place! They had also told me that it was customary to tip the door-person 50 Lire. I figured what the hell, nobody gets offended when you give them money, so without saying a word, I offered her a 50 Lire bill, and waited to be asked what it was for. Then I would run! Instead, she took the money, and asked me to come in.

It was a very large foyer, with marble floors, and a large circular marble staircase going up to the second floor. A very pretty lady in an evening gown was coming down those stairs, and she also greeted me with a very charming smile. She then asked me to step inside a room off the foyer, explaining that a client was leaving, and that they respected their privacy. After which, she asked me to follow her up the stairs. The door lady called her "Signora", so I figured she must be the madam. Her undulating backside mesmerized me as we climbed the stairs. It seemed to sway to the beat of some unheard melody, and I was in a total trance. Once on the second floor, she escorted me to a private room, asked me to make myself at home, closed the door, and left. It was classically furnished, with paintings on the wall, red and gold wallpaper, and sculptures on the end tables. This was the classiest place I had ever been in. Then the madam returned with four young ladies that seemed to have just stepped out of a glamour magazine. Each dressed in a different gown; they looked as if they were going to a ball. I was still mesmerized, and when the madam asked if I wanted to see any more girls, I just shook my head. I couldn't trust myself to speak, and I didn't know how much more I would be able to take of this. I pointed to the girl with the prettiest smile, and everyone else left.

The girl asked me to follow her, and once again it was up the circular staircase to the third floor. I figured the guys who came here would have to be in good shape, considering all the stairs they had to do. Her room was as tastefully furnished as the rest of the former "palazzo". She tried to make conversation, but I was just awe-struck, and only nodded. I sat on the bed, not knowing what to do next, and she slipped off her gown. In that moment, my life flashed before my eyes! All those girly magazines I had looked at; all the talk Roddy, Richie, and I had fantasized about on 243rd Street; what all that kissing was supposed to lead up to! My system was overcharged! When the young lady came over to help me undress, it was all over as soon as she touched me!

As I said at the beginning, it's not my intention to go into the nitty-gritty details of my awakening, but in retrospect, I found this very funny, and I'm leaving out the nitty-gritty; Except to say that the lady was a professional, didn't laugh at me, and patiently waited so that I could leave my virginity with her. After I left, I'm sure she told the story to her friends, and I'm just as sure it ended with, "What did you expect? He's an American."

\* \* \*

## Mike and I bike to Trani

Back in Corato, life was boring. We visited the relatives on both sides of the family, and went to an occasional movie.

It was strange to see American movie actors speak perfect Italian, and it took some getting-used-to. Plus, the seats weren't upholstered, and not comfortable by American standards. Also, the movie was shown in two parts, with an intermission. During this time, the lights would go on, and the young people would socialize, commenting on the movie or whatever else might be on their minds. The fact that they might be carrying on a conversation with someone that was sitting at the other end of the theatre didn't seem to present any problem for them. Kids would go around selling cold "gassose" for refreshment. In a town where everyone knew everyone else, it was a loud party time. That is, until they became aware that the "Americani" were in their midst! Then, there would be some toning down, until the word was spread and everyone knew where we were sitting. They weren't at all embarrassed to stare at us, like we had just landed from outer space. It was embarrassing for us, and it was a relief when the lights went off, and the movie resumed. To be fair, these were mostly local farm-boys, whose lives consisted mostly of work and home, and who rarely left town. With limited resources and education, going to the movies was a big deal. Having the "Americani" there was like having a bonus entertainment, and something to talk about later at home.

With all this time on our hands, one day I decided to do something different. I rented bicycles for Mike and me, and we headed for Trani, which was about nine miles away. We could have taken the bus, but I though a bike ride would be more fun. It was a nice ride on a sunny day, mostly downhill or flat. Arriving in Trani, I was struck by the difference between the towns! The people didn't all look like farmers! There was a large piazza, and more gardens and flowers, especially in the Villa Comunale, which overlooked the sea. We rode to the spiaggia (beach) that I remembered as a child, and of course that had also changed, except that it was still a sandy beach.

I couldn't wait to get back to Corato to tell my mother about Trani. Unfortunately, going back was not as pleasant as it had been coming. Now it was either flat or uphill, because Corato is about 1300 feet above sea level. I found it tough, and Mike was also having a hard time. A couple miles outside of town, there was a very long uphill climb, and we were already tired. Mike wanted to rest, but I was afraid that if we stopped, we'd wind up walking the rest of the way. I told Mike to try as best as he could, and that I would wait for him at the top of the hill. I struggled, huffed and puffed my way up, using the full road to zig-zag and make it a little easier to climb. When I finally made it to the top, I looked back to see how far back Mike was. I was surprised to see him maybe fifteen feet behind me, with a look of determination on his face, and staying right with me! He was determined to keep up with his big brother! The kid never ceased to amaze me!

I also thought about playing some sports, but they only played soccer, and that was totally foreign to me. However

I was told that there were a couple of basketball teams in Bari, and one day I took a bus to investigate. I found that the Sporting Club was right by the bus stop at the entrance to Bari. When I walked in and asked about playing on their basketball team, you would think that some high priced American professional basketball player had just come through the door. Obviously, being an "Americano" was a good thing if you were a basketball player. People came out the woodwork to check me out, and were falling over themselves to answer my questions. I was surrounded by perpetually grinning kids and adults, who showed me around. I saw the open-air court, surrounded by stands, and was told that the next practice would be in the evening of the following day. I thanked them, and said I would come back, dressed to practice with them. I felt like a celebrity, and couldn't wait to come back and show my stuff.

I was very excited when I came back the next evening, but surprised at the turnout of people who had obviously come to see "L'Americano". I was flattered, but nervous. What had I gotten myself into? I had never seen them play. Was I going to embarrass myself, and wind up being laughed off the court? Fortunately, it turned out that this was a category C team, and in my range of ability. The team welcomed me, and said that league games wouldn't start for a couple of months yet. So, once or twice a week, I would go to Bari to play basketball, and be treated like a basketball star. It was great for my ego.

## Meeting the Dammaccos –

One day, while sitting around with my buddies in Corato, I was told that other Americans had arrived in town. I asked how they knew that. Well, the pipeline had it that two girls had been seen riding bicycles on the "Stramurale" (a street that circled the outside of town). So what? Well, the girls were wearing pants! No proper girl would ride a bike in anything but a skirt, so they must be Americans!

As ridiculous as that may sound, they were right! A few days later, I was buying pastries, when a man introduced himself to me in English, and said that his sister and family were visiting from America. He invited me to come meet them, and gave me directions. Oh, to speak to some Americans again, especially kids my age. I told him I would be over that evening.

I had no trouble finding the place. It had no sign on it, but the building had a "pastificio" (macaroni factory) on the ground floor, with apartments on the upper two floors. The man sitting outside the front door told me it was the right place, and rang upstairs to tell them I was coming. I found out later that he was Leonardo Mastromauro, the founder of the pastificio. Upstairs, the man from the store, Nunzio Mastromauro, greeted me. Inside, he introduced the rest of the family, as well as the visiting Americans. Sure enough, there were two older girls, as well as an older brother my age, and a baby sister, as well as the parents. That's how I first met Mike and Mary Dammacco, and Mario, Aida, Angela, and Maria. They were as excited to see me as I was to see them, and we spent a lot of time comparing notes. Where we came from, how we liked Italy, etc. I had never heard of Long Island, but it was close to New York, and that was good enough for me. We parted, and agreed to get together again sometime, but it seemed like we had said all there was to say.

We had come to Italy primarily for business, and my mother was doing all that was possible. She had met with the accountant who had managed the building since we had left ten years ago. He was also one of the tenants. Surprise, surprise! The rents had remained the same, even though inflation had gone up ridiculously. She met with an attorney, and found that the laws favored the tenants. Rents couldn't be increased significantly, and it was almost impossible to evict tenants. She had gone to court to try to free one of the apartments for our personal use, showing that we were living in the storage rooms, but that wasn't going to happen. The best advice received was to sell the apartments. However, since the apartments were already occupied, a buyer would have to wait for the tenant to move, or sue as we were doing. It was definitely not a seller's market. The best prospects were the tenants themselves, who had a vested interest in staying put without going to court. However, they were living almost rent-free, so why should they shell out a lot of money to buy the apartment. It had to be a good deal for them. I mention all of this to show that the selling of the property was a tedious affair, with lots of talk and negotiating, leaving lots of free time on our hands. Actually, my mother was doing all the tedious business. I was too busy trying to amuse myself, and have fun.

Clockwise from top: With Mario; With Franco; Mario, Aida, and Angela at the Pastificio; The villa we rented; "Dining" at the villa; My mother, Mike, Vito and Isa.

So, with summer at hand, my mother agreed to go to Trani to see if we could rent a place for the summer. After taking a bus, we rented a horse-driven carriage to drive us around town. Riding along the "lungomare" to the beach, we saw the Dammaccos standing in front of a villa. We stopped and chatted. Amazingly, the villa belonged to Nunzio

Mastromauro, and had been built above the rooms that we had rented in the '30s. The rooms were still there, used as storage, and sitting on the rocks by the water. We let the carriage go, and while my mother socialized, Mario introduced me to the neighbors from across the street, the DeTomas. They had a very large property, and a son our age named Franco. Actually, they had ten children, with Franco being the oldest. He was very friendly and outgoing, and invited us in to see his place. He told us that the small villa on the grounds was their summer place, and escorted us to see the rest. It had an empty swimming pool, an unfinished tennis court, and a large villa under construction. Only the basement walls and ground floor had been completed, but it was obviously going to be big. The DeTomas were just as obviously rich, and I was very impressed. More so, when Franco took us down to the unfinished basement and showed us the ping-pong table he had there. He asked if we played, and when we said no, he proceeded to play a game with his brother Rino. They were very good, and I made a mental note that this was a game I wanted to learn to play.

When we left, we agreed that it would be nice to spend the summer in Trani, socializing with the Dammaccos. My mother found and rented a place on Via Colonna very near the Mastromauro villa. It was part of the Villa DeCristofaro, but apart from the main house. It wasn't much to look at, but it was on the waterside of the street, with a great view, and steps that would take us down to the "scogli" below. It was a modest place, with a couple of rooms, but it was like Heaven compared to where we were living in Corato. Later in the summer, we moved to a larger villa. It wasn't on the water, but it had fruit trees and grapevines on the property. Even better, it wasn't far from the villa where the Dammaccos were staying, which belonged to Leonardo Mastromauro, on Via Bisceglie. So, while I was doing my thing, my mother socialized with the Dammaccos, and Mike had his own little group of friends, including Franco's little sister Pompea, who really liked him. The rental used up almost all the money that my mother had gotten from the building in Corato, which was after expenses from the accumulated rentals from six tenants for the previous ten years. It was a really poor return on the investment. Fortunately, the dollar exchange was very good, and we were getting a lot for our money. Not that my mother ever discussed this with me, but it certainly seemed that we were living within our means.

## Entrance into a New World

That summer was a fabulous time! It was like I had stepped into some kind of fairyland, some kind of dream-world, and I didn't want to wake up! Every day was something new, every day a new feeling, and it felt like I had finally arrived where I wanted to be the rest of my life.

It started with the morning breakfast. Fresh rolls and bread were delivered right from the bakery by a kid on a bike. My mother would pick fresh fruit to go with the bread and jam. She roasted coffee beans to try to make a more

American-type coffee, and it was great. After breakfast, down the road to pick up Mario, and see what we were going to do. We would then go down the road some more to see what Franco was doing, usually joined by Aida and Angela.

Just as usually, Franco had been up for hours, and was not home. He was spear fishing, swimming the waters across from his house, with snorkel and flippers. We would wait for him to come out, and it was a sight when he did. He was in good shape, and looked like some kind of sea-god as he strolled out of the water; Snorkel up on his head, spear gun in one hand, and a few fish in a net in the other hand, walking awkwardly until he removed his flippers. He would show off the fish he had caught, and then we would decide what to do. Most times we would go swimming off those same rocks. The water was clear, and the rocks warm to rest on. Other times, we would go to the beach.

Franco was a major influence to us. He knew everybody. Through him we met all the other well-to-do kids in town. What made him such a great guy was that there was not an ounce of snob in him. He was comfortable in his own skin, and was at home speaking to a fisherman or to the mayor. Although he was friendly with everyone, he didn't have any real close buddies until we came along. His family was from Brescia, and had a winery in Trani, bottling table wine under the family name.

Clockwise from top: Aida; Paola Malcangi, Mario's dream girl. Also Laura Guacci, and Nino DiPantaleo. He had no money, and her parents didn't approve of the relationship. They eloped, Franco driving them to Naples to get married; Gida Albanese, Mario's 1st dream girl; Aida, her 1st crush Vladimiro Falcone, Angela, and Nanni Albanese, who was Gida's sister, and my only dream girl; Titi Germinaria and Isa Plantulli; Partying at Franco's villa.

*   *   *

So, we had entry into a crowd of people like: Isa Plantulli, the mayor's daughter; Paola Malcangi, daughter of a nationally known lawyer; Cataldo Malcangi, her cousin; Nicky Mongelli, the son of Senator Mongelli; Vladimiro Falcone, son of the bank director; Mario Porro, an old and respected family; Bice Guacci, daughter of one of the largest marble foundries in town; As well as others, like Matteo DiChiano, who were also industrialists, or like Gida Albanese, the daughter of an accountant. These people were in a different universe from those in Corato, or from any other that I had ever met. Boys and girls socialized freely, and they seemed so knowledgeable of world affairs. They knew more about American history than I did. The girls participated in all discussions, and they especially impressed me. The American kids that I had known seemed very shallow by comparison.

It would be naive for me to say that it was all because Mario and I were so wonderful. Being American certainly had its curiosity factor, but that would have worn off pretty quickly. The guys certainly wouldn't welcome more competition with the girls, and the girls saw us as a novelty. It was Aida and Angela that made the difference. They were very pretty girls, and you couldn't get them without getting us. Especially considering that the parents were very strict, and Mario had to chaperone all the time. It follows to ask why I wasn't attracted to them. Well, I was, but not in a boyfriend way. They were certainly pretty, but I had seen Mario as my friend first, and it wasn't right to think of them as anything else other than friends. Besides, spending so much time together, they were like family, and I came to see them as such.

The next question would be, what did I contribute? While the Dammaccos were really Mastromauro, they had a macaroni factory in the family and related to lots of money. The Mastromauros were also well known in the community, if not universally respected, but that's a topic for another day. I was just me. It happened that Mario and I bonded very quickly, even though we had totally different characters. These experiences were as new to him as they were to me, and we would review each happening from the perspective of two American kids in a foreign land. It was exciting to get together with the Dammaccos for these sessions. Where we didn't discuss much personal stuff in my family, these people talked about everything, and talked, and talked, and talked, maybe too much! However, the kids didn't speak Italian, and I served as translator while they were learning. Not that I spoke it that well, but the double-duty made me improve much faster. Another benefit gotten from the Trani crowd was that they all spoke more Italian than dialect, as did their friends visiting from other parts of Italy. This made it possible for me to learn the language with a minimal local inflection. I like to believe that I was accepted because I was a good guy. Plus, Franco told me that Trani had its own basketball team in the same league as the one from Bari, and that he was a player. He introduced me to the team, and I was welcomed, much as I had been in Bari. That helped make me more attractive in the group, and more popular in town.

I would have no trouble writing hundreds of pages on my summers in Italy, and I would still not do it justice. So many things to say, so many feelings felt and seen, that it would just wind up being confusing and boring to the reader. So, I will keep them to myself to review at my pleasure, and just write about some of the experiences that stand out in my mind.

As I said before, it seemed like I was living in never-never land. What a life! Wake up in the country, have breakfast of fresh rolls, butter, jam, and fresh fruit, with American style coffee that my mother would roast and brew. Then off to the beach, to talk, swim, and play with "la comitiva" the crowd. Sometimes, plans would be made to have a dance over at someone's house that evening, and arrangements had to be made to have a record player and records there. Most times, we would agree to meet in Piazza Bisceglie, where we would spend the evening walking, sitting, and talking. In the mornings, after the beach, it was home to eat and sleep for the afternoon. With a few exceptions, everything shut down for the afternoon, and reopened around 5 PM. It was the hottest time of the day, and air conditioning was unheard of. It was amazing how quickly I adapted, and looked forward to my afternoon nap. Afterward, I would wash and dress for the evening in shirt and slacks. I loved those Italian shirts! Whether we spent the evening in the Piazza, or at a movie, or dancing, it was always something to look forward to, and to talk about when it was over.

I've been saying "I" in describing my day. Actually, "I" didn't do anything without Mario, and most times Aida and Angela accompanied us. It was like we were joined at the hip, and Franco was the next closest. We were the Three Musketeers, and when you got one of us, you got all of us. We got around on motor scooters. Originally, Franco gave us a lift on his Vespa. Eventually, Mario and I got our own scooters, both Lambrettas. Mario's was the deluxe LC, which he maintained like it was a Rolls Royce, while mine was the standard model, and I loved the sound of its motor.

As I hinted at before, the attractions of the "comitiva" for us were the girls. Although some were already coupled off, there were those that were as "available" as we were, and that made up 99% of the conversations with Mario. He really liked Gida, and his whole day was spent trying to find out if she liked him as well. In the beginning, as a translator, it kept me very busy. Then, we would discuss the day, and see if he had made progress or not. Her apartment overlooked the Piazza, and we would sit on a bench in the evening that had a clear view of her balcony. There we would sit to see if she came out, or if she would come out to walk in the Piazza. With Mario, he was either in agony or in ecstasy! Gida was very pretty, bubbly, and easily the most popular girl in the group, both with boys and girls.

Initially, I liked everybody. I didn't have a preference other than Gida, and she was off limits. So, I enjoyed the whole group, although I did have an uncomfortable experience. "Titi" was a good-looking girl, with the sexiest walk I had ever seen. The legs would go one way, the hips another, with the body following in a delayed reaction. She was also considered to be a free spirit. Anyhow, one evening Titi and I found ourselves alone walking in the Villa Comunale, along the darkened paths that overlooked the water. We sat on the wall and made conversation about all sorts of things. It was a beautiful night and I quickly realized the romantic possibilities. I just as quickly realized that I didn't know what to do! I was afraid that if I tried to kiss her, she might say no. How embarrassing. On the other hand, if I did kiss her, then she would be my girlfriend, and I couldn't fool around with the other girls. On the other hand, if I didn't try, she would think I was just a stupid American. On the other hand, how "far" was it proper to go in Italy. All these things and more were going through my mind as we talked. To put off the decision, I smoked one cigarette after another, offering to her as well. Eventually, I ran out of cigarettes, as well as any courage to do anything. We realized nothing was going to happen, and walked back to the Piazza. We remained friends, but I never got another chance.

Near the end of the summer, Gida's older sister Nanni came to visit for a few weeks. She was residing in Rome. I was smitten by her delicate beauty, but was told that she was "fidanzata" to somebody in Rome. Nevertheless, I looked forward to seeing her at the beach, or have her walk with us in the Piazza in the evening.

Aida and Angela had their own crushes on Vladimiro and Matteo, and Cataldo Malcangi later on, but they didn't have the freedom that Mario and I had. That didn't stop them from talking about them. As a matter of fact, time spent at the Dammacco house was time spent scheming. It was a totally new experience for me.

The summer passed, and we returned to Corato; The Dammaccos above the Pastificio, and us to the rooms in our building. However, Mario and I would make almost daily trips to Trani on the scooters, and we continued to be part of that group's activities. Without the beach, there was much less to do, but we tried. Sometimes Franco would have a get-together at his empty villa, since his family had also moved back to their main house in town.

One time, Franco, his brother Rino, Mario and I, had a full meal and a little too much wine at the empty Mastromauro villa. There were always the evening walks, and occasionally gala dances at the "Circolo", the club where the well to do got together. It was a luxurious place, taking up a full floor in Malcangi's building in town. It had a large hall for dancing, with marble floors, big chandeliers, and a bar. As impressive as the place was, I was even more awed by the behavior of the people. There was a lot of bowing and hand-kissing. I had only seen that in the movies, although there were some titled people in Trani, such as Baron Bianchi, and some very old families. Attendance at these affairs was very restricted, but we got in because of Franco, as usual, who was accepted everywhere. He simply took us along as his guests one night, and we were OK from then on.

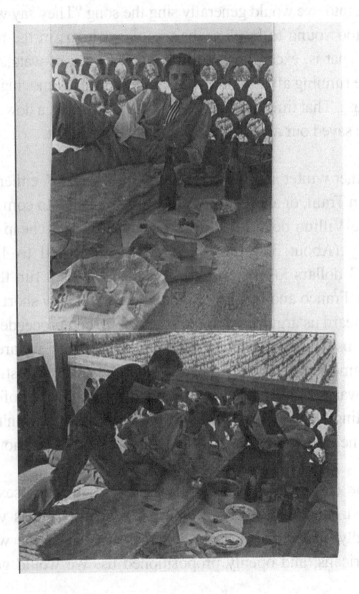

Invariably, after these affairs, Mario and I would return to Corato on his Lambretta late at night. We would first get fresh-baked pastries from the "Sette Nani Bar" (this was before Bar Centrale). Then we would stuff newspapers under our jackets, as a buffer against the chilly night. On the nine mile trip back to Corato, we would generally sing the song "They say we're just too young to love" at the top of our lungs in the night sky. That is, except for the time when a pack of watchdogs came running after us, and the Lambretta wasn't moving fast enough. That time, we just screamed! Fortunately, a downhill slope saved our asses, which were being nipped at.

Another winter activity was visiting the "casino", either the one in Trani, or another town. They didn't begin to compare to the Villino delle Rose in Bari, but they were cheap and handy (About 300 Lire/1 dollar, as compared to 1000 Lire/3 dollars for the Villino). Besides, it was a fun thing to do. Franco and I picked the odd ones. One very short girl overheard us arguing in the waiting room, and proceeded to show us that between the crotch and the armpits, we are all the same height! Once, Franco and I argued over a prostitute that was so fat, that when we stood on either side of her standing sideways, we couldn't see each other! I won't go into the discussions on the way home, but it was hilarious.

At the casino in Trani, there was a resident homosexual named Felice, who was like the handyman. He was very friendly, lusted after Mario and myself because we were Americans, and openly propositioned us. We would goad him on, saying the other homosexual in town was better than him. This would get Felice all riled up. He would insist that Guerrino was nothing but a hairy beast. When challenged to prove it, he would drop his pants to show that he shaved his rear end daily, and was very proud of that fact. When we would run into Guerrino in town, we would tell him what Felice had said. With a sniff of disdain, Guerrino would say that Felice was nothing but a prostitute, while he only did his thing with those that he loved. He would then proceed to open the big locket that he carried on a gold chain around his neck, to show the picture of the love of his life: An American Army Captain from the period of occupation during World War II. He would then go on to suggest that he could fall in love with either one of us. That's how we got our kicks!

In the picture, I had arranged for Felice to sneak the girl I wanted out of the Casino. This was against the rules, and they both could have gotten in big trouble. We went riding on the scooter, out with Franco on his sailboat, swimming at the spiaggia, and had a very enjoyable afternoon. After which, I brought her back to Felice, and he sneaked her back into the house, in time for the evening trade. No, there were no charges. This was personal time!

We had gone to Italy to sell the properties, and the Dammaccos also had a reason for going that year. This would probably be a good time to review their story.

## The Dammacco – Mastromauro Story

Leonardo Mastromauro brought his family to America, but his dream was to have a macaroni factory in Italy. They settled on Long Island, and they all initially got jobs at the Sunshine Bakery factory in Flushing; Even the youngest daughter Mary, who falsified her age because she was too young. Eventually, Leonardo returned to Italy to follow his dream, and the family continued to work in America, and send money to him. He started making macaroni in small quarters, and would set the pasta to dry in the sun, outside in the street. He would then put the pasta in wooden crates, load it on a horse drawn wagon, and go around town, selling it to the Salumerie (grocery stores). Eventually, as he got more business, he called his sons back. His oldest son Franco decided to stay in America because he had started his own successful business, the Sunshine Coal and Ice Company.

Back at Sunshine Biscuit, Mary fell in love with a new worker, Mike Dammacco. He had been working on an Italian freighter, but jumped ship in New York. He was good-looking and dashing, and she was hooked! Unfortunately, the rest of the family didn't see him that way. Let's just say that they really didn't like him, and even tried to get him deported.

In any case, Mike and Mary married, and their marriage was a rocky one all the way. He was a great guy, and loved his family, but he had a very short temper, especially after a few glasses of wine. Being unskilled, he had worked for a while with Frank at the coal and ice company, but it didn't work out. Mario remembers that Frank screwed his father out of the business. Mike had his own truck, but Mary would make calls to get him jobs. She also did other work to bring in additional money. They lived from hand to mouth, and Mary on occasion would have to hock her wedding ring to buy food or go on vacation. In spite of this, when they would entertain friends, or play cards, Mike would share whatever he had. If Mary objected, he would get physical with her. With all that, he was her only love, and she especially loved dancing the tango with him, which was also very entertaining.

This was the atmosphere that the kids grew up in. It affected Mario and Aida the most, and they have remained extremely money-conscious their whole lives. They remember earning quarters at the cemetery, by getting water for the people at the gravesites. They remember hiding food under the bed when company came, so that the father couldn't give it away. They remember wearing used clothing that they got from customers. However, they also remember happy times, and recall their childhood memories fondly. The fact was that the Dammaccos were entertaining, but short on money.

Fast forward to 1950. Leonardo Mastomauro had evolved his dream into the Pastificio Riscossa, and was on the verge expanding once again. However, he had never forgotten how he had started, and how his daughter had worked and sent him her earnings. He invited her and her family to come to Italy, with the intention of giving her a share in the Pastificio. However, the feeling wasn't unanimous. The brothers felt that they had made major sacrifices, helping to build the Pastificio, and suffered through World War II, when their lives were at risk due to the shortage of food in the town. They were not willing to give away a share to the sister, especially since they still didn't like Mike.

There were some heated exchanges that summer, and at one point Leonardo announced that if his daughter didn't get a share in the Pastificio, he was going to padlock the doors, and stop all production, until she did.

That broke the logjam, but not the acrimony. While discussions were going on, there must have been some especially nasty things said, because one morning I ran into Mike Dammacco in Trani, and he told me that he was leaving the next day. He said that they could take the Pastificio and shove it, and I was very impressed that he could walk away from such a deal, just on principle. I didn't know their whole family history at that time, other than that he was a truck driver in the States. Sure enough, the next day he was gone, leaving his family behind. A couple of months later, he was coaxed into returning, but it was clear that he was not happy in the role of the guy who was married to the daughter of Pastificio Riscossa. Although the in-laws didn't like him, the workers did, as they saw him as one of their own. He was a very natty dresser, and very fastidious about his appearance. He also was from Bari, so he was a local boy.

Getting a share in the Pastificio didn't turn out to be a total gift. Mary got a share, but she had to pay for it. Since they had no money, it was agreed that it would be paid out of her share from future earnings. Since they were rebuilding the Pastificio, future earnings would be severely reduced, and while the brothers had other income producing holdings, Mary was totally dependent on the Pastificio. Nevertheless, it was much better than anything they had had before, with a better future. Also, she was useful to one of the brothers.

Attilio, the baby of the family, had devoted his whole life to the Pastificio, and was its chief technician, for which he received an extra 10% off the top of the earnings. This didn't make the older brothers Nunzio and Giuseppe happy, and there was friction between them. Mary tended to side with Attilio because of his expertise, and this evened out the two camps. The other brothers also competed for her vote, so she was in a pretty good position. The stories of the Mastromauro family would require another book, and it's beyond the scope of my writings. It's enough to say that the Pastificio Riscossa was the financial salvation of the Dammacco family.

## Bar Centrale - Pasticceria Povia

The next summer, my mother rented an apartment in Nunzio Mastromauro's villa in Trani. It was great! Right on the water, with Franco across the street, and the Dammacco's just down the road. Plus, my mother and brother had lots of company to socialize with, while I was out playing. The good times continued, but with a new twist. Because of the Korean War, I had been sent a notice that I had been drafted. We went to a doctor in Corato, got a letter saying that I was sick and couldn't travel, and sent it to the draft board.

In the meantime, the occupants of the apartments realized that they were going to have to start hiring lawyers to defend themselves, and that it would be to their advantage to buy the apartments they were living in. Whatever the reason, they began to make offers to our attorney, and eventually deals were made to sell all the apartments and the stores beneath them. My best memory is that we wound up with about 13 million Lire, or about 40 thousand dollars.

It was at this point that my mother decided to invest part of that money into a local business. I assume that she had gotten my father's OK, figuring that it would be a reason to retire in Italy. It could also have been a reason to keep me in Italy and out of the draft, but I don't see how. I just don't know the motivation for sure, but she started asking around about business opportunities. It turned out that a local merchant and the town's best pastry man were forming a partnership to open a Bar and Pastry Shop outside of Corato, and they were willing to accept another partner. We went together to look at different possibilities, but it seemed that none satisfied the merchant. His favorite saying was that we should not rush into things and that we must have "piedi di piombo" or "feet of lead". It soon became clear that he also must have had lead up his ass, and that we weren't going to do anything with him around. So, together with Gino Povia, we made a deal to take over a bar in the center of Trani. Gino was about seven years older than me, but very talented. He also wanted to do things first class, and the original estimate of investment wound up doubling, amounting to over half of the money gotten from the sale of the apartments. My mother wanted to hire my uncle Amerigo for the Bar, but Gino didn't agree. He pointed out that Amerigo had no pastry experience, would be there only to look after our interest, and couldn't see why he would have to pay him a salary. It made sense, so my mother put her brother in as manager, and paid him out of her share. She gave him a salary of 100K Lires a month, compared to the 60K Lires he had been making as a chauffer, and a move up the social ladder. That may have been another reason for the investment. Unfortunately, she and Mike returned to the U.S., and didn't get to see the opening of the Pasticceria Povia. I remained behind, but I didn't know for how long.

From the Top:

Bar Centrale

Opening Night Blessing and Ceremony. Carlo (on left, next to Archbishop), and Giovanni (2nd from right), were our super-duper waiters.

At opening of Bar Centrale, with Gino Povia.

At opening, Bar counter. At left is Riccardo Rella. He started with us as an assistant barman. Over the years, he proceeded to become a main barman, then an excellent waiter, then learned the pastry-baking end. Years later, after we closed, he opened up his own bar and pastry shop, and called it the Bar Centrale. It was the best in town. Unfortunately, his kids didn't like the business, and it died with him.

Bar side room

At opening of Bar Centrale, with Mario and Franco. At left is Franco's brother Rino, and the owner of the FIAT agency in Trani.

Bar Centrale in the summer, with plants and outdoor tables.

\* \* \*

This would be a good time to talk about the Bar. Located in the center of town, on the fashionable corner of Via Mario Pagano and Via San Giorgio, it was an instant hit. Gino had redone the Bar both inside and outside with marble floors and a marble façade. The main bar room had a long impressive refrigerated counter; with a huge espresso machine, and an elegant glass display case for pastries. Mirrors and neon lights made it look even bigger, and the back wall was framed by a backlit, glass-etched and colorful mermaid. It was very attractive, and people would come in just to admire it. There were also two adjoining large rooms, with tables and chairs, where people were served during the winter months. As soon as the weather was warm enough, the tables and chairs would be placed outside, where we had space for at least thirty tables. Behind the bar were three other rooms, the "laboratorio" where the pastries and gelato were made. The opening was a gala affair, attended by all the local dignitaries, with the Mayor and Archbishop cutting the ribbon.

Gino's reputation had preceded him. His pastries were delicious, and would just melt in your mouth. The gelato was creamy, and the "torta gelato" was his unique specialty. The quality was far superior to anything else in town, and the Bar Centrale became a magnet for people to go to, both for the product, as well as to see and be seen. It wasn't unusual to have a hundred people sitting outside on any given evening, and there was constant traffic all day. The parents of my friends were regulars, and I developed my social skills interacting with the customers. I would also take my turn at the cash register, help out in the "laboratorio", do some of the shopping, and try to make myself useful. However, Gino made the final decisions, and we were all just a supporting cast, which was fine with me, since I didn't know anything. In short order, because of our reputation and connections, we were offered the Bar concession at the "Circolo", the private club for the well to do, where Franco had introduced us. The following summer, we were also given the Bar concession at the beach. Later on, we also got the rights to operate "La Lampara", a summer open-air nightclub above the beach, which was owned by the Tourism Club of Trani, and was listed in the tour books.

Gino had studied to be a master pastry chef, which included making some tasty meals. So, he was also in demand to cater weddings, and people would come from the surrounding towns to enlist his services. Unfortunately, we didn't have enough tableware or personnel to take care of the demand, but we took on as much as possible, and sometimes more. The stories of how we stretched a service for 100 to accommodate 300 may seem funny now, but caused great anxiety at the time.

Given all of the above, you would think that we were rolling in money, and you would be wrong! The reason for both our successes and our difficulties was Gino.

From the beginning, too much was spent on renovating the Bar, so that we opened already in debt. Then, with each success came additional need for equipment and supplies, which created more debt. Also, Gino didn't want to turn down any prospective business, and would cut his prices dramatically rather than lose a catering job, to the point that we had some jobs that we actually lost money on. While this may have been OK at the beginning, when we were getting established, it wasn't justified later on. As I became more knowledgeable, I tried to talk some sense into Gino, but he was obsessed with getting his name out as much as possible.

It was amazing how much stuff was being produced out of the "laboratorio", to the point that we would run out of room to put the product on, both in the back and in the front, until it was taken away to some job. At the end of a hectic day, after all the returned tableware had been tabulated for breakage and loss, we would sit around in the back like drunken sailors, amazed at how we had been able to accomplish what we had that day. The truth was that, in addition to Gino and his staff, it wouldn't have been possible without our two top-notch headwaiters, Carlo and Giovanni. They were excellent, and could make a staff of fifteen people work like one of forty. Carlo was our fulltime employee, and Giovanni was the headwaiter at the local hotel, but available to us for all occasions. They knew they were good, were like prima donnas, and always argued with each other when they worked together. Ideally, it worked best when each would have his own crew at separate affairs, although then they would argue afterwards about who had done a better job.

It would have been easier if everybody paid up front, but that wasn't the custom, especially with the well to do. It was funny (not really), that when we catered weddings for farmers or working people, they paid the regular price, and settled the account in full at the end of the evening, with much appreciation. The judges, attorneys, professors, industrialists, etc., not only bargained down to the lowest possible price, but didn't pay at the end, and would insist on a further discount when they eventually decided to come in settle their bill.

So, it wasn't surprising that we soon found ourselves in a squeeze between our suppliers and our customers. After we had gone delinquent on a couple of payments, they refused to ship unless we signed a personal note, called a "cambiale". If this wasn't paid when due, the supplier could shut down the Bar, and put a lien against it. Every day became a doomsday! We would check the cash available, and the debts to be paid. There was never enough cash, so we would begin to separate those who could be put off. If that still wasn't enough, we would start telephoning those who owed us money, or send Carlo out to make the rounds to collect what he could. Sometimes we were still short, so we would contact the director of the bank that was holding the notes, asking him to hold them until the next day. Since they were also our customers, they tried to help. Sometimes the next day was no better, and the bank would send it to the "notaio" to start the process. I remember a few times getting to the notaio just before he closed for the day, to pay off a cambiale. It was a terrible way to live, and left me shell-shocked. Of course, it didn't happen every day, but it was often enough to leave a lasting memory. To give Gino his due, he sometimes would take on a losing proposition, just to generate some revenue to pay some immediate bill. Of course, it just made it more difficult for the future, but that was a problem for another day. In spite of the difficulties, Gino and I got along very well, and he was a very hard worker.

\* \* \*

Besides all the other goods things that I was enjoying in Trani, I was also playing basketball, and getting some very good write-ups. Of course, being an "American" basketball player made a difference, but I was also pretty good.

We won the championship for the "Serie C", beating the big team from the big city of Bari. It was quite a feather in the cap of a small town like Trani, and there was a brief deliberation by the sporting club about moving up into the next category. They decided against it because it would have been too expensive, but we had made our mark.

In the off-season, we hosted a tournament, where we invited a team from Austria to play on our court. They built special stands, dressed it up with ribbons, and the mayor and the "in" people were invited. Of course, all the kids of those people were in our crowd, and it was show-off time for me. I wish I could say we won the game, but we didn't. Lost by a couple of points, but we lost. Nevertheless, I had my fans, and I couldn't go anywhere in Trani without being hailed. As a matter of fact, even fifty years later, during the summer in Italy, I ran into people that remembered seeing me play. Very satisfying.

\* \* \*

With all the properties sold, we had no place to go back to in Corato, so we stayed in Trani. We got more involved with the Mastromauro family, which wasn't always a good thing. That summer is memorable to me for two occasions.

## The night Nunzio was "kidnapped"

One evening, we were socializing with Nunzio's wife Lina at the villa, when we heard screaming from her upstairs' apartment. We all rushed upstairs, and found her son Dino screaming that his father was missing and that he must have been kidnapped. A quick search confirmed that Nunzio was not in his bed, and nowhere in the villa. We knew that whoever took him couldn't have used the stairs, because we were there inside an apartment with an open door. The only other way out was from the balcony, down to the enclosed entrance to the villa, and the villa's gate was closed. As serious as the moment was, images were made that were later found to be hilarious, and to be retold many times through the years. Like teenage Dino, jumping up and down in his underwear, screaming over and over that his father had been kidnapped "Hanno rubato mio padre". Then, in a moment of inspiration, he turned to their dog Lola, and urged her to go find "papa'". The dog of course didn't understand a word, but started barking and running around in circles. In the meantime, the wife Lina had worked herself into hysterics over her missing husband, but her screaming without her upper dental plate was not a pretty sight. The only one who didn't seem to be affected at all was the younger daughter Nietta. She just stood by the doorway, taking it all in. At least, until her mother became aware of it! At which point, she went to the daughter and screamed, "What's the matter with you? They've kidnapped your father, and you just stand there? You don't laugh, you don't cry, what's the matter with you?" The outburst was accompanied by a couple of heavy slaps to the poor girl's face, which of course made her cry. This seemed to satisfy Lina, who then said emphatically, "That's better!"

With all this confusion going on at the same time, I figured I needed to get some help, so I took my scooter over to the Dammacco villa, and they all came over promptly. It was agreed that this needed to be reported to the police (carabinieri) right away, and we accompanied Lina there to make a report. The kids stayed at the villa, and Mary went with Lina to the police. Mike Dammacco, like myself, just didn't feel that a kidnapping was possible. There had to be another reason. Because the Mastromauros are a strange bunch, we decided to go to Corato and check the apartment over there. When we got there, he went upstairs, and after a while, came back down, shaking his head and laughing. Nunzio indeed was in the apartment, together with a young female, and couldn't understand what the fuss was about. He said he had gotten an "urge" after going to bed. So, he dressed and sneaked past us out of the villa, picked up a female acquaintance, and brought her to the apartment in Corato. He said that he would tell Lina that he had just remembered some work that he had to do, and had left quickly without telling her. As ridiculous as it sounded, that was the story he wanted told. So, leaving him behind, we raced back to Trani, and to the police station, to assure his wife that all was well. Lina was still there, crying and telling all who would listen about what a wonderful man Nunzio was: A devoted and loving husband and father. A man who lived only for his family, and who's only other passion was his work. A man in a million, admired and respected by all, etc. She was carrying on and on, when we arrived and gave her the good news, as Nunzio had told us. Without missing a beat, her hysterics turned to rage! That wonderful person she had just been describing was transformed into the son of a whore, who was no better than a piece of shit stuck under the sole of your shoe, and that was one of the nicer things she had to say about her husband. We got her out of there and back home, and we all went to bed. It must have been three in the morning. Sure enough, Nunzio came back the next day, stuck to his story, and couldn't understand why she had made such a big fuss. For them it was normal, for us it was a classic remembrance.

The other memory is much shorter, but it could have been serious. One evening, I was riding in a car with some friends, just cruising around with no particular destination. Riding along Via Colonna, we passed the villa where we were staying, and one of my friends asked me, "Isn't that your little brother riding your scooter?" I looked, and sure enough, there was Mike with my Lambretta, with a friend on the back seat. He was trying to ride the scooter along the street, but it kept stalling on him. I asked to stop the car and got out. I was a couple of hundred feet away when Mike saw me coming, at which point he bolted from the scooter and ran for home, leaving his friend holding the scooter. I ran past the stalled scooter, and chased him to the villa, but he got in and hid on me. My mother didn't know what was going on, and she wouldn't tell me where he was. I was very upset, not because he had taken the scooter without permission, but because he didn't know how to drive it! There was a drop from Via Colonna to the rocks below, and he could just as easily have driven off the edge. My mother stayed calm, and pointed out that thankfully he didn't get hurt and she was sure he had learned his lesson. I think he did too, because I understand he was so scared he had the runs for the next three days.

It just so happened, that although we had agreed on a partnership with Gino Povia, the place in town was a long way from being ready. However, he had worked a deal to operate a summer open-air bar on Via Colonna, and we put our partnership into operation. It turned out to be the basement of the villa we were at, owned by Nunzio. It opened up on the side street that led down to the water, with a beautiful view. It was right next to the storerooms that we had rented back in the 30's (It's on the right side in the top picture). Gino and I went to Naples, and came back with a pizza-maker. We had blue neon lights put in, and called it "La Grotta Azzurra", The Blue Grotto. It was a bar-pizzeria, and soon became the place to go to in Trani. The pizza was good, and Gino's gelati were even better. However, nobody liked Gino's gelati or whipped cream more than Mike. He was always hanging around to get some, and could never get enough. One time he went too far. Waiting at the machine that made the ice cream (It's on the right side of the bar, in the middle picture), he became impatient, and decided to reach in and get an early taste. His arm got caught in the vat, and jammed the mechanism. Fortunately, the power wasn't strong, and we were able to get his arm out without any damage to him. It was my first involvement in a business, and I found it very exciting.

Now we needed more permanent quarters, and my mother found a place in town. It was called Villa Fasanelli, and it was bigger than we needed, but my mother must have gotten a good deal. It was a large villa with spacious rooms and grounds. We moved what little furniture we had from Corato, and settled in. A few months later, she realized that she had no more reason to stay in Italy, and made plans to return home. Her return trip was from LeHavre in France, and Mario and I accompanied her and Mike on the train ride to the Italian border. There was a delay because she didn't have a visa to enter France, and we had to go back to Torino to get things squared away, but they left without further incident.

Back in Trani, Mario and I found new ways to amuse ourselves. The one we enjoyed the most was getting to the casino before it opened at 9AM. We figured that since we were the first that day, and the ladies had been resting all night, they were like virgins at that time. Eventually we realized that it wasn't sound reasoning, but it took a while.

That summer was memorable for another reason, Mario had gotten over his Gida infatuation, and was now smitten by Paola Malcangi, who he considered to be way above his reach, if for no other reason than the name and the wealth. As luck would have it, Gida's sister Nanni (my infatuation) came to spend the summer in Trani, and we saw quite a bit of her. I don't remember how we did it, but we managed to arrange to play canasta (just the four of us) at the Malcangi villa one afternoon. What an experience! What a luxurious villa! We sat at a card table in a beautifully decorated room with marble floors, and served by the houseboy in white jacket and gloves. Paola and Mario. Nanni and I. I felt like I was performing in a movie!

We pushed our luck, and asked them if they wanted to come with us on our scooters the next afternoon, to go see a movie in the next town of Barletta. We told them we would wait in the Piazza for them the next afternoon, but we didn't expect them to show. Paola on a motor scooter? Never happened! Nanni was engaged to a guy in Rome, for crying out loud! So, you could have knocked us over with a feather when they both showed up the next afternoon at the appointed time. I think we floated to Barletta, and my body tingled where Nanni had her arms around me. We went to a movie, and on the way back there was a thunderstorm. We took refuge under a monument outside of Barletta commemorating "La Disfida di Barletta". I didn't care. It could have rained for a week! Eventually, we got home, and we only went out one more time. This time Mario borrowed the car, and we drove to Barletta for a movie. There was some handholding, but nothing more. Mario and I felt like fish out of water, Paola because of her family name and wealth, Nanni because she was engaged! I didn't know what the future held for me, and I was in no position to make any commitment. So, it didn't go any further, but Mario and I always wondered what could have been. I'm glad I behaved as I did, especially after Franco DeToma told me that Nanni had asked him if I was someone who could be taken seriously, and he had backed me. That could only mean that it was possible that she would have broken her engagement for me. Whew!

It wouldn't be fair to pass by this period without mentioning the ladies' great attraction to Mario. He was a beautiful guy, and the girls went ga-ga over him, especially the older ones! The older ones would actually proposition him. For example, and industrialist and his wife were visiting at the Mastromauro villa. The man's young and pretty wife showed a keen interest in Mario's Lambretta. Claiming that she had never ridden on a motor scooter, she convinced him to take her for a ride to the beach and back. At the beach, she guided him to a secluded spot, where she proceeded to manhandle him. He was self-conscious and nervous, but cooperated fully. However, they didn't have much time. On the way back from the beach, she asked him to stop by her villa the next day. When he did, she said, "Ahhh, now we have more time".

Another time, a very attractive woman introduced herself to him on the beach, and made it clear that she was available. Nunzio and family were in Corato, and nobody was at the villa. He took her there, and they didn't get out bed for 24 hours, or so he told me. They didn't see the insecure guy that I saw, who was always looking for reassurance. I have to admit though, that with time, he came to accept his gift, and made the most of it.

Nothing like that ever happened to me, although I had no shortage of girlfriends. No pretty women propositioned me, and I was afraid to do anything serious with the girls that I knew. For example, I had a very pretty girlfriend named Rosa. I allowed myself to get involved with her because she was not part of our crowd. She was my date when we had the get-togethers at the empty villas after the summer, and great company. At some point she said that her parents wanted to meet this guy she had been seeing for a while. That seemed fair enough, and I agreed, but when I got to her house, I couldn't go upstairs. To me, it was like a declaration, and loss of my freedom. I turned around and left. That night I told her it was something I couldn't do, and I never saw her again. I just wasn't ready for anything other than fooling around.

**The Bar Centrale – Pasticceria Povia** had it's grand opening during the winter, and it was a gala affair. It was by invitation only, and the mayor and the Archbishop did the ribbon cutting at the entrance. All the top families attended the cocktail party, dressed for the occasion. It was a great night for Gino and me. Also attending was a priest by the name of Schiraldi. I'm sure he wasn't invited, because he had a bad reputation, as someone who brought very back luck. Just the mention of his name would cause people to immediately start scratching their private parts, because that's the best way to ward off the evil spirits. I'm telling you, it was a sight to behold! Here was a gathering of rich, educated, and influential people, enjoying themselves. As soon as padre Schiraldi was seen coming smiling through the doors, expressions changed. All the men left their wives, or groups that they were having conversations with, so that they could scratch themselves privately. Some hadn't taken off their coats yet, but it was clear what they were doing, and it was hilarious to us nonbelievers. I didn't see the women reacting or doing anything, so it must be a guy-thing.

Everyone seemed to have a Schiraldi story, and a few years later I would have my own. In 1957, Aida and I were on our way from Trani to Corato in our car, and she was pregnant with Marco. While stopped at the train crossing in Trani, padre Schiraldi (excuse me while I scratch myself) approached and asked for a ride. Aida didn't know about him, and I was a non-believer, so I figured what-the-hell, and asked him to get in. We had gone no more than about four kilometers, when I see a rider-less wagon coming towards us in the distance, the galloping horse wandering all over the road! Not having enough time to turn, I pulled as far over to the side as I could, hoping that the horse and wagon wouldn't come barreling into us. Fortunately it didn't, and Aida became very agitated. So, I turned the car around quickly, and followed the galloping horse and wagon, blowing my horn to alert people of the coming danger. This made it even worse for Aida, and she was almost in hysterics by the time we were back at the train crossing. Fortunately, the DeToma house and winery was there, and I pulled into it. I got Aida upstairs, where Mrs. DeToma got her calmed down. I don't know what happened with the horse and wagon, but when I went back outside, padre Schiraldi was still waiting by my car, wondering if I would still give him a ride to Corato. I asked him to get other transportation, and have scratched myself ever since.

Sometime before the summer of '52, the Dammaccos returned to the United States. The reason was that there was not enough money coming in from the Pastificio because of the heavy expenses involved in the building of the new plant, and they needed to go to work while the value of their share increased. After we had seen them off at the train, Franco and I decided that it would be a great idea if we followed them. We knew they were going to stop off in Rome for a day or two to visit Gida, who was there visiting her sister, and we imagined what a big surprise it would be when we showed up. Without a second thought we jumped on my Lambretta, and headed for Rome, 400 miles away. In those days there was no super highway, and we had to cross the Appennines towards Naples before heading up to Rome. It was after midnight and we had gotten only as far as Ariano Irpino, a town high in the mountains, where the road was so steep that they had cut notches in it so that tires could get some traction. The Lambretta struggled, but made it into town. However, it was cold, and we weren't dressed for the weather. Plus, we were tired. So, we drove the scooter into the railroad terminal, and got some sleep on the wooden benches.

We got to Rome by the next evening, and tried to contact Gida, without success. It was only then that we realized what a stupid thing we had done. We had no clue as to where anyone was, and what to do. So, we decided to stay the night, and return to Trani the next day. We had left in such a hurry that we had not brought official identification, a requirement when checking into a hotel. We were fortunate to find an understanding clerk, and that Franco's father's name wasn't Vincenzo. It seems the police were looking for that Franco DeToma. In the picture is Franco, next to my Lambretta.

The next day we left for Trani, but took the long way back to sightsee, and stopped off in Naples for a day. It was a stupid and tiring trip, but we enjoyed it. Franco and I became closer buddies, and we spent a lot of time together. With my mother and Mike gone, I spent a lot of time at Franco's house, and I became like another son to them. All those kids! Franco was followed by Rino, Isabella, Pompea, Gianni, Michele, Lorenzo, Antonio, Raffaella, and Nicola. I understand they had also lost a couple as infants.

There was always commotion in that house, and every meal was like a party. Pasquale DeToma was a character right out of a movie script. With bushy eyebrows and loud voice, he made his presence felt. His wife Pasquina was quieter, but with strong convictions, and seemed to be the real boss. Pasquale would go to bed with one opinion, and wake up with another. One classic example was Franco's attempt at getting some independence. Since he was his father's right-hand, he asked for something that he could call his own. His mother wanted him to wait until all the children were adults, but Franco pointed out that by the time that the youngest would be 21, he would be in his 40's. He had started to bottle the wine, and was selling it in a small store that he had opened in Trani. All he asked was that he be allowed to keep that as his own. Since I was spending so much time there, I was allowed to help plead his case, and we would spend many evenings talking about it. Occasionally, Pasquale would be convinced, but when he came out of the bedroom the following day, he had reverted back to his wife's opinion.

Otherwise, Pasquale was a dynamic and forceful person. One classic story is worth recording. He was in a lawsuit with his family on business matters, and one day decided to attend the proceedings. He sat in the back of the court, and listened as his attorney presented to the judge papers showing that he had paid what was due. The opposing attorney objected, pointing out to the judge that those so-called payments had been made by check, and what was the guarantee that Pasquale DeToma had the money to back up those checks? At this affront to his name, Pasquale jumped out of his seat, and approached the bench. Pulling out his wallet, and taking out a wad of money, he pleaded with the judge, "Your Honor, how much would it cost me to slap this person around? I'll pay anything, and it'll be cash!" This last part he said while standing over the cowering attorney. Eventually, they got him calmed down, but the story made the rounds.

Another time he was shopping in Bari with most of the family, when he got the urge to attend an opera. Pasquina pointed out to him that they had all the little kids with them, and that they weren't properly dressed for the opera.

To which he replied, "Those who know me know I can afford proper dress, and I don't care about those people that don't know me." Of course, he used much more colorful language than that. I found him to be a very colorful man, and he liked me, as did his wife and children.

One time I tested how much they liked me, but not by design. They were celebrating a family occasion, and I was invited. They set up the dinner table in the formal dining hall, which was rarely used. Mrs. DeToma took out her prized hand-embroidered tablecloth from her trousseau for the occasion, a single cloth to cover a long table sitting about thirty people. Together with matching napkins, silverware, crystal goblets for water and wine, silver candleholders, under a sparkling crystal chandelier, and with the serving staff standing behind waiting to serve, it made for a beautiful picture. It was another one of those moments when I felt like I was in some kind of fairyland. I was honored to be included in such company, but also very intimidated. We sat for dinner, and I made it through the champagne toast. I looked to see what silverware others were using before I committed myself, and I tried to make conversation, but I was nervous as Hell. Fortunately, Franco sat across from me, and that made it easier. Unfortunately, my nervousness betrayed me. Reaching for the goblet of wine, my fingers slipped, and the glass spilled the wine all over that beautiful and precious tablecloth. There was an audible gasp from those seated nearby, and I prayed that a hole would open up and swallow me. There was a momentary silence that seemed like an eternity, and then Franco came to my rescue. He reached out and tipped his own glass of wine over. Now there were two very large stains, and what had been a disaster turned into something very funny. With much shaking of heads and smirking, the older members carried on about "these kids", but without malice. However, I wasn't reassured until Mrs. DeToma took me aside and convinced me it was OK, that it would wash out, and that after all, it was just a tablecloth! She wasn't as kind to Franco, because he did it on purpose, but I'll be forever grateful to him. Great guy.

I really feel like I need to move on. So many memories, such a turning point in my life, I could go on and on, but I think I've done enough for now. Since this is a work in progress, maybe I'll come back from time to time to add other stories. Besides, I don't want to start rambling.

## My Military Service: 1952-1954

As I may have mentioned before, I had been getting letters advising that I had been drafted for military service, and to report for my induction. We had responded advising that I was unable to travel because I was not well, accompanied by confirming notes from our friendly doctor, but the letters were getting more insistent and threatening. Besides, there was really no good reason for me to stay in Italy. I was living alone, the Bar Centrale had opened, and uncle Amerigo was our representative there. He brought his wife and son to Trani, and moved into the villa that we had rented. I didn't have much to do, and I wasn't looking forward to spending the winter there. Besides, I was involved in a relationship with Emelia DeCristofaro, the daughter of the landlord of the villino that we had rented on Via Colonna in 1950. We had spent the summer dating exclusively, and I was afraid that I would have to make some kind of declaration, especially since the family knew me, I was a friend of the brother, and we occasionally went out with her married sister. She came from a family of lawyers in Bari, and her father was a judge. We had done some "heavy necking", and I was afraid that at some point we would go over the line. I wasn't ready for that, and it was time to leave.

I booked passage from Naples, and said my goodbyes. Franco volunteered to drive me to Naples. Mario Porro decided to come also, as did the senator's son Nicky Mongelli and a few other buddies. We left Trani during the night in two cars, and made excellent time. So much so, that we arrived in Naples early the next morning. Since the ship wasn't scheduled to leave until the late afternoon, it was decided to take a ride south to Positano. I had never been there, and was curious to see it. What I didn't know was that the road of the Costa Amalfitana skirted the outside of the mountainous region, full of tight turns, with a drop-off to the water below. I noticed that occasionally, niches had been dug into the side of the mountain, with the statue of a Saint inside it, surrounded by fresh flowers. I noted that Italians must be very religious, to put these stations in such out-of-the-way places, but I was told that was not the case. Each niche was put across from the point where someone had driven off the road and been killed. That had a chilling effect on me; especially on the return from Positano, a beautiful town that everyone should see. The two cars decided to race each other. That was scary enough for me, but Mario took it a little further. He pulled out the hand throttle, and stood up on the seat of the car, a Giardinetta that had an open roof. He told the other passengers to also stand up, and to throw their weight on the other side of the car on the turns, as a counterweight. Fortunately, I was in the other car with Franco, and although he stayed in his seat, the others stood up, and also acted as counterweights on the curves, whooping and hollering. I stayed seated, and was scared pickles. I was sure I wasn't going to see the ship, and wondered how these guys had all gotten so stupid all at once. They had never behaved like this before, especially Mario! Miraculously, we made it, and they saw me off. As the ship pulled away from the dock, we waved to each other, and I realized that a major chapter of my life had come to an end. It was sad and troubling, because I didn't know what the future held for me.

Top: Death-defying car ride on Amalfi Road; Taking a break.
Bottom: Last view as my ship left: My "shipmate".

Fortunately, the sadness didn't last long. There were some foreign exchange students coming to America, and I had a cabin all to myself. There was a Greek girl that I had a hard time getting out of my cabin, but I tried to get to as many others as I could. It was a fun trip. The most surprising thing was the self-assurance that I had developed. I was definitely not the same person that had left the States. I was comfortable, and able to make intelligent conversation with people of all ages, but more important, girls were chasing me, instead of the other way around. Thank-you, Trani.

It was great to be home, and I enjoyed getting together with the old crowd, but I found the same difference as on the ship. My Florida and Italian experience had put me a quantum leap ahead of my buddies who had never left the neighborhood. I saw them as kids, and their wonder and questioning about my life only reinforced that feeling.

Unfortunately, the government also had been keeping track of my activities. Apparently monitoring all incoming passengers, they were aware that I had returned home. How else to explain why, three days after my arrival, I received a letter telling me to report at once to FBI headquarters in Manhattan. When I did, I was given a notice of immediate induction into the Army, unless I failed the physical exam. About ten days later, I presented myself at the Whitehall Street headquarters, passed my physical, was immediately inducted, escorted to a waiting bus filled with other unfortunate souls, and driven out to Camp Kilmer in New Jersey to begin serving my two-year term of duty.

Once over the shock, I saw Army life as another adventure. It was something like my Florida experience, living and sharing my life with guys my age, the big difference being we were going to be trained to go fight a war in Korea. That part hadn't really sunk in on me yet. I was more fascinated with the fact that they were putting saltpeter in our food. Since we were restricted to the base, and living in such close quarters, the Army didn't want the boys to get frustrated or make unnecessary "tents" during their sleeping hours. At least that was the scuttlebutt. I got the impression the boys were frustrated just because they couldn't make "tents". We got our uniforms, supplies, haircuts, shots, etc., and Visitors' Day was about a week later. My mother, father, and Mike came to visit, after which we were bussed down to Fort Lee, outside of Richmond, Virginia, to begin our basic training.

Four weeks of weapons training, and four weeks of classroom for a designated specialty. Here I got my first break. I was designated as a supply specialist, and not an infantryman, which reduced my chances of seeing action by a lot. So, with that reduced anxiety, I was able to better concentrate on enjoying the service to my country. With my buddies, I would go to the USO dances, and try to pick up some of the local girls. This wasn't hard to do, since that's why the girls were there, mostly hoping to meet someone who would take them out of Richmond. I made it clear that I wasn't in the market for anything serious, and I also did OK, without violating the principle that I had established in Italy; No sex with "nice" girls. Whenever I got the urge, there was an elevator operator in a Richmond hotel that would fix me up. I also found a great Italian restaurant, and had quite a few meals there.

We also weren't far from Washington D.C., and would sometimes drive there for the day, just to look and fool around. Such things as stopping the car, and one of us jumping out and up on one of the statues, just to have a picture taken while waiting for the light to change. Couldn't get to sit on Lincoln's lap in his monument because of the guards, but we did leave a tour of the Capitol, snuck out one of the windows, and took a picture under the flagpole that's on the roof of the entrance. I don't think that would be possible today. One time, we left late at night, and encountered a very dense fog. We didn't want to miss reveille, so we took turns sitting on the hood of the car, and hand signaling directions, using the white line as a guide. It was a fun group.

After basic training, I qualified to go to Leadership School, and I took advantage of it. It delayed my getting shipped out for another four weeks. This consisted of my getting an acting sergeant's rank, and being in charge of the recruits in one of the four buildings of the Company. I had my own room, and answered only to the Master sergeant, and the Company Commander. It was very competitive, and my group was number one almost every week. I had them marching in all different directions, and then come back together again, like some kind of precision marching monster, and everybody enjoyed it.

My crowning achievement though, was my class on "gray propaganda". While addressing my class in the shade of a tree on the parade grounds, the master sergeant ran across and whispered something in my ear. This had been prearranged. I then told the class that the Korean War was over, and that they were going to go home tomorrow. Bedlam broke out! When I finally got them settled down, I told them it was a lie, and an example of gray propaganda, which is to believe something only because someone in authority is saying it. Think for yourself, and question! If the War indeed had been over, would the Master Sergeant whisper it only to lowly me to tell you? The Company Captain was standing right there: wouldn't he have known before the sergeant? Especially in wartime, all kinds of rumors make the rounds, especially in the service, and we need to be more discerning. The class was properly impressed, as was the Company Commander, who said nice things to me.

All good things come to an end, and I eventually received my orders. I was given two weeks vacation, after which I would be shipped to Korea. Finally faced with this reality, I met with the Company Commander to explore possible alternatives. I pointed out that being in a service unit, I would be serving in the rear echelons, and most likely not see any active duty. I was much more qualified to serve in

Europe, and I also stressed that I had abandoned a personal business in Italy to come and serve my country. He set me up to meet with the chaplain, who then arranged a meeting with the JAG (Judge Advocate General) office, who then set me up to meet with the Officer in charge of assignments the following day. I spent a good part of that night polishing and repolishing my brass, spit-shining my boots, and otherwise preparing to make the best impression possible. When I presented myself in my most starched and properly creased uniform, I was sure I couldn't have done any better, and I got the impression that it was noted. The Captain listened to my story, and was sympathetic. He asked a clerk to see if I could be replaced by someone else, and was told there was no one. I thought that was it, but my favorable impression came to the rescue. After being quiet for a couple of minutes, the officer told the clerk to change my specialty to one that could be replaced, and my orders were changed to go to Europe! I floated out of that office, and felt like I floated all the way to New York to begin my two-week vacation before I would leave for my European vacation. It was great to be home, without having to look forward to going to Korea. My parents were also very relieved, and we enjoyed our time together.

I shipped out on the "General Buttons", which wasn't anything like the ocean liners that I was used to. Upper and lower hammocks were hung up in large open quarters, and the ship rock-and-rolled across the Atlantic, landing in Leghorn (Livorno), Italy a week-or-so later. There I had another shot at getting a better assignment, trying to qualify as a linguist, and staying in Italy, but this time with no luck. I was given an office job at the Regimental Quartermaster Headquarters of the 350th Infantry Regiment, stationed in Salzburg, Austria.

## An impossible coincidence

The train ride was memorable for an impossible coincidence, one that I still find hard to believe. On one of the stops before the Italian border, I lowered the window from our compartment, to look out at the traffic on the station platform. A vendor, pushing a cart filled with pillows for weary travelers, stopped and looked at me with a puzzled look. Then, he got all excited, and started jumping up and down, pointing at me and shouting, "Tu sei l'Americano, tu sei l'Americano!" I thought, "Well duhhhh, of course I'm the American, considering I'm wearing my Army uniform, on a train full of American soldiers." I figured he was going to a lot of trouble just to sell me a pillow. No, no, he said. I was the American that he had seen play basketball in Trani the year before. Now it was my turn to be shocked! What are the odds? He went on to tell me that he had been working at the Hotel Jolly, and had come to every game. He was a big fan of mine, knew that I had a Lambretta, and used to look for me in town. We talked about some of the games, and he gave me a pillow, but wouldn't take any money. I was surprised and flattered, to say the least.

We got to Salzburg, Mozart's birthplace, and were bussed to Camp about thirty minutes out of town. What a picturesque city! Surrounded by mountains, with a river running through it, and a castle overlooking it, with distinctive and unique dwellings. It was a living, breathing postcard. It hosts the renowned yearly Salzburg Festival, and is a great tourist attraction.

The Army camp was just an Army camp. We were restricted to the base until we were indoctrinated; Being advised about the people, how to behave, what was expected of us, etc. Also, we could not use our regular dollar currency. We were paid in so-called "script" dollars, which was only good at military facilities. We were forced to exchange it for local currency before leaving the base. This was so as to keep the amount of dollars collected by a foreign nation to a minimum.

## The "Indoctrination"

We couldn't wait for restriction to be over, so that we could get into town for some "action". We heard so many stories from the "veterans". However, since we couldn't go to the "action", the "action" came to us. One of my buddies told me to go take a look at the fence that surrounded the camp. After dinner, I went and saw the damdest sight! There, spaced maybe fifteen feet apart along both sides of the cyclone fence, were soldiers and prostitutes facing each other, in varying stages of negotiations for services. For those couples that had reached an agreement, the prostitute would turn, bend over, and back into the cyclone fence. The soldier would then have to find the appropriate opening in the fence to consummate the deal. It was getting dark, but visibility was still good. In my life, I have never seen a more unique sunset! I passed on the opportunity. It was just too gross!

Top: With Jerry Lyons. Read about his
"trial" further down; My office.
Bottom: Leaving office; On weekend break in
Mondsee, Austria. Jack Kelly is in background behind
me. There will also follow stories about him.

I had expected a vacation, and it was. I was in the 350th
Infantry Regiment Service Company, and assigned to work
in the Regimental S4 (Quartermaster) office. My office
was above the regimental warehouse, where we worked a
regular 8-5 shift Monday through Friday, and were bussed
to and from the office. Of course, reveille was at six, and
we had the usual military chickenshit to put up with, but
it was a small price to pay. I thought I had it made when I
found that my office boss's name was Captain Domenico

Delli-Carpini, but he wouldn't talk anything but business, and that was also our relationship. Maybe if I had been an officer, it would have been different. However, I wasn't a private for long. My Leadership School training, and overall performance got me the first promotion in my group. After the minimum period of three months, I was promoted to PFC. I had some good buddies. Mike Danze from Brooklyn, and Bert Treble from Honeyoe N.Y. were my closest, but there were also Joe Rossi from Chicago, Jack (Irongut) Kelly, and Jerry Lyons from Michigan, as well as others whose names I don't remember right now. We worked together, and went out together. Salzburg had a USO club, and no shortage of bars and clubs that welcomed American servicemen. There was also no shortage of Austrian women willing to extend their type of welcome. What was shocking to me though, was the number of beautiful blond blue-eyed girls coupling up with negro soldiers. I felt that like should go with like. I felt that everyone should have an equal opportunity in life, but I didn't extend that to include interracial romance. Logically though, where else were these guys supposed to go? Besides, the girls were in it mostly for the money, and maybe a chance to get to America through marriage.

Weekends we would generally go out of town. In the summer months it was to Mondsee, a small town on a lake, near the German border. It was great because it was our private place. No Americans. We would rent sailboats for the day, and drink beer at night. We would sneak out a tin of coffee from the warehouse, which paid for our room and board. This was where I dethroned Jack Kelly as president of the General Paf Society, which was a beer-drinking tournament. To be honest, I had had previous experience in Trani, except that there it had been called the Cardinal Paf Society, and was done with double shots of anisette. Much tougher Society!

Other times we would travel to Berchesgarten, which is a short distance from the Eagle's Nest, Hitler's Hideaway in the Bavarian Alps. There was a luxurious hotel up there called the General Walker Hotel. Formerly, this was where dignitaries would stay before going up to see der Fuherer. Now it was for the exclusive use of American personnel, at very reasonable prices. It had a very large outdoor ice-skating rink, and a great nightclub with live entertainment. The views were magnificent!

As you can imagine, we always ran out of money before we ran out of things to do. Then we would stay in camp until the next payday. Movies were cheap, and I took advantage to improve my ping-pong game, as well as my pool table skills, at the recreation center. Also, American entertainers would come provide free shows, and politicians would visit to make sure we were being treated OK. I remember seeing different dance troupes, as well as Eddie Fisher, and speaking to Adam Clayton Powell. Another one of those strange coincidences happened one day at the movies. They were showing an episode of Candid Camera, and I almost fell out of my chair. It had been shot in the Mt. Vernon City Hall, and the victim was my Oculist, Abe Karash.

Occasionally, we would feel guilty about living in Paradise, while others were putting their lives on the line in Korea. However, nobody ever felt so guilty as to volunteer to go there. Generally, we resolved the problem by drinking beer until the feeling passed. Besides, it could have turned ugly for us at any time. It was during the Cold War, and our relations with Russia could have soured at any time. Down the road, the Austrian capital of Vienna was divided among the four Allies; American, English, Russian, and French. The representative MP's from each country traveled together to keep order. They even made a film about it, called "Four in a Jeep". There were always reports of "incidents" with the Russians. As a matter of fact, when we took the train to visit Vienna, the windows were shuttered when traveling through Russian occupied territory. It was believed that they didn't want us to see all the tanks that they had ready to go. Maybe that was an example of gray propaganda? We met a few Russian soldiers at the Luna Park in Vienna, and had some intense electric bumping-car fights, but that was it. They were kids away from home, just like us, with the same curiosities. We exchanged views, and cigarettes, and had a good time together. Their cigarettes were funny. Same length as ours, but two-thirds of it was a hollow tube without a filter. Before lighting up, they would pinch the tube together at one point, then rotate it 90 degrees, and pinch it again at another point. Although the tobacco length wasn't much more than an inch, it was so slow burning that it lasted longer than our cigarettes. When we got back to camp, we inquired as to what we were supposed to do if the worst were to happen. We were told that we were expected to fight a delaying action while we got the Hell out of there. Sounded good to me, but it still made me nervous every time we went into the countryside on maneuvers to practice shooting anti-tank rocket launchers.

On maneuvers, doing KP With local kids

Top: Gida & Cataldo Malcangi Bottom:
Nanni & Future husband on the left

We also had thirty days vacation per year, and I used that time exclusively to go to Trani. I had been gone less than a year, but it seemed so much longer, and it felt like I was going home. It was great to see the "comitiva" again, as well as my uncle Amerigo and Gino at the Bar Centrale.

I also got to see my boxer "Geronimo" again. I had left him as a puppy with Mario Tarantini, and he was now full-grown. He recognized me instantly, and bowled me over. The days passed quickly, and it was a sad day for me when I left. Actually, I was sad and broke, with only the train ticket to get me to Salzburg, which was how I got to experience that unique Italian personality.

**A taste of the Italian personality**

It was my first return trip, and I had assumed that the trains ran 24 hours a day. Maybe so, but the connections weren't. So, when I pulled into Rome at 1:00AM, I found out that the next connecting train to Austria wouldn't leave until 8:00AM. While I was wondering what I could do to amuse myself for the next seven hours, I was approached by a boy who couldn't have been more than fifteen years old, who addressed me in English, "Joe, can I carry your suitcase?" Considering I was in civilian clothes, I was startled and surprised to be recognized as an American. I always thought I could pass for a native, considering the time I had spent in Italy, but my duffel bag gave me away. Anyway, I thanked him in Italian, and told him to try to help someone else, because I was broke. After a brief hesitation, the boy put on a hurt expression, and said in Italian, "Joe, I have a cousin in Chicago, and someday I'm going to America. You have no money? Don't worry. I'll help you. Come with me". With that, he took my duffel bag, and led me out of the train station, to a row of taxicabs that were parked there, waiting for fares. He went straight to the group of drivers that were standing around, introduced me like a long-lost relative, and stressed that I was broke. They immediately all adopted me, and led me across the street to a Bar. There they insisted on buying me a cappuccino, with a pastry, and whatever else was available, like I had just come in from the desert. After which, back to the cab stand, where they assured me that they would keep me company until it was time for me to leave in the morning. As one would leave with a fare, another would arrive to drop off a fare. He would then join the group, and be updated on my condition. The new arrival would then offer to take me across the street to the Bar again. I was really thankful and touched by their generosity, but after a couple of hours, we had run out of things to say. So, once again thanking them, I told them I would go for walk to kill some time. After much handshaking and hugging, they let me go, making me promise that if I got bored I would come right back. I wandered around the deserted area, and stopped at a piazza across from the station. A Bar that had closed for the night had left the chairs and tables stacked outside, so I pulled up a chair and sat. There was almost no pedestrian traffic, but a prostitute appeared out of nowhere, and propositioned me. Once again, I briefly told her my story. Once again, I was confronted with, "I have family in America. Someday I'm going to go to America. I love America. Don't worry, I'll keep you company until you have to leave". With that, she pulled up a chair, and like two long-lost friends, exchanged histories. A pretty girl, not much older than myself, she had not been in the business all that long. Her story wasn't all that different from those that I had heard from other prostitutes in Italy and Austria. Poor family, small town, lost virginity for any number of reasons, and enticed by the money to be earned in the world's oldest profession. After an hour or so, we were so friendly, that I ventured to ask, "Look, I appreciate you losing a night's business just to keep me company, but since you've decided to do it, why can't we get comfortable at the same time? You said your apartment is nearby, why don't we go there". With a stricken look, she admonished me, pointing out that that was business, while this was personal. The illusion that they could have a respectful life separate from their profession was another trait that I found them to have in common. After a while, the sun started to come up. We hugged and wished each other well. I went back to the station to wait for my train, with a warm feeling for these people, and very proud to be of Italian descent. However, I was to still have another example of that Italian generosity.

We pulled into the station at the Italian border town of Brennero, and once again I had a layover of about four hours for the connection to Salzburg. Wandering around the town, I stopped in at a Bar, but I was still broke. A young man asked me if I was tourist, and in the following conversation found out about my destitute condition. He immediately asked me to follow him downstairs to meet his friends. Below the Bar was a restaurant, and four more of his friends. I found out that they were train conductors, and Brennero was the end or the beginning of their shifts. They insisted I sit and order a meal, and made sure I ate until I couldn't. When it came time to leave, once again it was with lots of hugs, like long-lost friends. The Italians! What great people!

I spent a year and a half in Austria, and almost two months of that in visits to Trani. Once I took my buddies Bert Treble, Mike Danze, Joe Rossi, and Jack Kelly with me. (In the picture, Bert is on the left, and Joe on the right. Pasquale and Gianni DeToma are on either side of me). We stopped off in Rome and Venice on the way down. They loved the country, and the unique experience of being invited to a full Italian dinner at the DeToma house, with all the kids. They had never seen such a feast, and everybody laughed when they pulled away from the table, thanking their hosts, saying they had never eaten so much in their lives. It was very funny because we had only finished with the antipasto. They were amazed to learn that the aperitivo, the wine, the soup, and the other tidbits served so far was supposed to build up their appetite, and that the main meal hadn't started yet. The pasta, the meat, the fish, the nuts, the fruit, the wine, and the pastries (with more sweet wine) that followed, was more than they ever imagined, and I'm sure left them with a lifelong memory. We had fun at the beach, and they were an entertainment for the "comitiva". I even took them to the Casino, and paid one of the girls extra to "take care" of Jack Kelly. Poor Jack! He came from a family of athletes, and before the draft, he was always in training. He had planned to try out for the next Olympics. Unfortunately, in the service, he started drinking beer, and going out with loose women. He often would say how glad he was that his family couldn't see him. I guess he should not have hung out with us. Anyway, I don't know what that girl did to him, but when he came out of the room, he was beet-red with embarrassment, but with a grin from ear to ear, and kept repeating "I can't believe the things she did to me. Oh my God, I'm so glad my family can't see me." He kept grinning all the way back to Austria.

While I'm on the subject, I should talk about Jerry Lyons' "trial". You see, while Jerry always came out with us, he always went back to camp alone after we had "hooked up". He was a virgin, and said he wanted to wait until after he was married to have sex. Well, we of course didn't agree with him, and spent quite a bit of beer-drinking time debating the issue. I got the idea to put Jerry on trial to see if his point of view had merit, and everybody agreed. In short order, we reserved a private room in back of the local bar, assigned a prosecutor and defense counsel, and chose a jury of his peers. Of course I was the judge, and my beer mug was my gavel. The word spread, and we had a great turnout. With much drinking of beer, arguments were presented for and against poor Jerry, and he was even put in the witness chair to answer some very personal questions, which would never be asked had we been sober. It was hilarious, and surprise, surprise, he was found guilty! The sentence was that he had to lose his virginity immediately. The good-looking waitress that had been serving us was honored to be his first love, and promised him that it would be memorable. She stressed the fact that she didn't normally do "these things", and took him to her quarters above the bar. However, we wanted a witness to the affair, and the "prosecuting attorney" volunteered himself. The three of them went upstairs for the night, and we went about our own business. The next day we were told what had happened. The three of them had shared the same bed, with the waitress in the middle. Although try as she might, the poor girl couldn't get Jerry to cooperate, maybe because he was a little drunk. After a while, she gave up. The poor guy on the other side had been forced to just watch, and he was more than willing to take Jerry's place, but the girl said no. She had said that she didn't do these things, and that she was making an exception for Jerry. She promptly went to sleep; leaving two guys awake for the night, one who wouldn't, and one who couldn't. The story made the rounds, and we were mini-celebrities for weeks.

Another story that's worth telling is about the time I accompanied Bert to visit a girl he had met somewhere, and gotten her address. It was near the camp, and we took a taxi over there. I had gone with him once before to visit another girl that he had met, and she had a girlfriend, and we had all wound up sharing the same bed, at the same time. Four people in a bed made for two didn't allow for sleeping time. I was hoping for the same result this time, except to have my own bed. Sure enough, she called her girlfriend from the apartment across the hall, and we spent some hours talking about everything. When it came time to go, she asked Bert to stay the night. Since it was very late, her girlfriend invited me to stay with her until morning. Graciously, I accepted, said goodbye to Bert, and followed her to her apartment. I should have known something was wrong when she didn't turn on the lights. She took my hand, told me to be very quiet, and led me across a darkened room to the door to her bedroom. As I was tiptoeing in the dark, I heard some very loud snoring. When we were safely in her room, she told me that we had just come through her parents' bedroom, which was the only way to her bedroom! My first instinct was to get the Hell out of there! Then I figured that I probably wouldn't be lucky twice in a row, and I had visions of being beat up by an angry father, with nothing to show for it. So, I decided to take my chances, and stay the night, figuring to get lucky. Unfortunately, here was another girl who "didn't do those things", even though she allowed me to share her bed. She had just been doing a favor for her girlfriend. I didn't understand it then, and I don't understand it now. It's just as well. I kept picturing the mother or father coming in to check on their daughter, and how I was going to handle it. Dawn came very quickly, and I decided to take my chances and leave. She said it wasn't a good idea, since her father was an early riser. The only other way out of the apartment was out the window, and we were on the third floor! There was a lot of snow on the ground, and a large mound almost under the window. I decided to take my chances, and jumped out, praying that the father hadn't gone for an early morning walk. He hadn't, and I didn't break anything when I landed. It was really cold, and I hurried across the farm that was next to the camp. I soon realized I should have taken the long way around the field. The farmer had recently "fertilized" his land, and the stink was horrible! I had seen those "Honey" wagons at work, distributing the human waste "fertilizer". I don't know what I stepped in, but when I got back to the barracks, no one would come near me. I had to put my laundry bag outside until it was picked up, and I don't remember how long I stayed in the shower, soaping over and over.

For the last six months or so, I had a more-or-less "steady" girl, Hilda Bier. She worked in an office on the base, and had a four-year-old son, Johnny. She had a sad story. It seems that she had married an American sergeant during the Occupation, and Johnny was their son. However, their marriage hadn't been approved by the Armed Forces, and she was not allowed to come back to the States with her husband. Although he said he was going to do whatever was necessary to bring her over, he soon changed his mind. He offered to bring over only his son, and when she refused, he never contacted her again. What a dirt bag!

I made no promises, and she was free to date whoever else she wanted, but we had fun together. We went to different places every weekend, but most times would leave the hotel room only to get something to eat. In spite of our understanding, she surprised me by coming to see me off at the station when I was rotating back to the States, and I can still see her crying on the platform as the train pulled out. We exchanged a few letters, and that was it. She said she was thinking of going back to her hometown, where there was someone willing to marry her, and adopt her son.

I hope it was true, and that she did. She was a good person and deserved better than what she got.

Before I close out my military service, I should mention that although I was the first to get a promotion, I was also the first to lose my stripe. I eventually got promoted again, only to lose it again. It seems I had a problem with sergeants. Work was fine, but back at the barracks, there were always little chicken-shit things being insisted on by the RA's (Regular Army) sergeants in charge. The closet and footlockers had to be just so, everything folded in a certain way, and they insisted on being treated with respect. Unfortunately, the ones in our company also happened to be very stupid, attaining rank only because of length of service. At the Quartermaster Regimental building, they spent their days in the warehouse, loading and unloading trucks, while we were at our desks in the air-conditioned offices above. So, back at the barracks, they would pull rank to show that they were the real bosses. The other guys were able to live with it, but I couldn't help some snide Bronx remarks. This was designed to get under their skin, and it did. Losing my stripe the first time was hard to take, because it meant I couldn't make sergeant before my enlistment was up. The second time it didn't bother me as much. I complained to the Company Commander, and he took me into his office, and closed the door. He agreed that I shouldn't have been demoted, but reminded me that I would be back in civilian life in a few months, while he would still be there, and he had to back the sergeants so as to make his own life easier. It seemed sort of spineless on his part to me, although I didn't say so. So, I went in a Private, and I came out a Private. I have no one to blame but myself. I certainly could have gotten along with those guys. They were not that bad. The Army was their life, and they lived within the rules. I, on the other hand, saw myself as a civilian, and superior to them, with a visible chip on my shoulder. I won't go into the troubles I had with the MP's (especially the short ones), and how close I came to getting locked up many times while in town. It would also explain why I never heard back from the Officer Review Board. When I was still a model citizen, my Company Commander had recommended me for Officer Training School (or something like that) to become a 2nd Lieutenant. I appeared in front of a panel of Officers for an interview, and obviously failed. Maybe because they asked me to sit down and relax, and I did (I should have remained standing). Maybe because my answers reflected that I would not follow all orders without question (a big no-no). Anyway, I never heard from them. Just as well. A military career was not for me.

## On the way back home

On my return home, we again stopped at the camp in Livorno for processing. I should mention that it was about the same group that had come over. We had been assigned to different companies, and had not seen each other since. One of them was Jack Reynolds, and his family owned a restaurant/bar on Lake George called Indian Kettles. I didn't know where that was, and I didn't imagine then that I would get to see his place.

Although restricted to camp, I talked another buddy into jumping the fence that night. Dressed in civilian clothes, we went into town, wandered around, and hit a few bars. I figured that speaking Italian would get me to meet some fine women. Didn't happen. So, I got a taxi driver to pick up a couple of "good ones" for us. It was dark, and I wasn't in very good shape, so it wasn't until we were in a hotel room that I realized how ugly my "maiden" was. Besides ugly, she was short, stout, had a great mustache, and only one breast! Strangely, the first thought that came into my head was, "Franco should see me now. I bet he would really fight me for this one".

When we got back to camp, we got caught while we were jumping the fence to get back in. An Italian Carabiniere saw us, and since we were in civilian clothes, whistled for the MP's. I caught a break when the sergeant on duty recognized me from when we had come over eighteen months before. I had been on his work detail. Good sergeant! He told us to get lost. The trip home was uneventful. Figuring correctly that discipline would be pretty lax on the way back for a bunch of guys getting out of the Army, I borrowed a buddy's shirt, and passed myself off as a Corporal. This put me in charge of work details, with access to the food supply. Pigged out on ice cream, and worked on a suntan. Nice trip.

Back home, we got processed out at Camp Kilmer in New Jersey. Once again, as of Sept. 4, 1954, I was a civilian, and except for my mustering out pay, I was broke.

## Back in Civilian Life -

I was welcomed back like a conquering hero, and it was great to see the family again, although changes had occurred. Mike was now a teenager, and had followed me to Cardinal Hayes High School, with much better success than I. He was still a really nice kid, and very helpful to my mother. My mother had decided that cars were better than trains and trolley cars. So, she had enrolled in driving classes, gotten a license, and talked my father into buying a car (a two-toned Dodge). Considering that she had never driven in her life, and was over fifty years of age when she decided to do so, I thought it was a fantastic accomplishment, and I still think that. She tried to get my father to learn, as did I, but he was totally uncomfortable, and wanted no part of it. He was satisfied to sit and give directions, and to let people know that it was his car.

I would say that the main reason for my mother getting a driver's license was because of the continued friendship with the Dammacco's. When they had come back from Italy, they had stayed at our house for a couple of weeks, until they got settled in their own place out on Long Island. To go visit them took a long time by trains and buses, so a car was almost a necessity. In the picture, it's Mario with our mothers.

Mario was still in the service when I came home. He also had lucked out, by being stationed in Okinawa, working in the office as a draftsman. In the neighborhood, Richie had been excused from military duty because his father had died, and he was his mother's only child (or something like that). He had made the most of his opportunity by getting his degree in Engineering, and getting married to Jeannie. He may have gotten married, and worked while getting his degree. I'm not sure, but I didn't see much of him. However, I was honored to be the godfather at their daughter Barbara's Baptism.

Roddy's mother had died, his father remarried, and Roddy couldn't accept the change. Maybe it was because he found his father to be more caring towards his new wife than he had ever been with his first one. Maybe because the new wife was trim and perky, while the previous one was grossly overweight and sickly. Whatever the reason, Roddy had spent little time at home after his Army service, going out drinking and partying. Apparently, he met and married someone on one of his binges. At least that's what I heard, because I didn't see Roddy when I came back.

Left to my own devices, I decided to take advantage of my GI Bill, and start my college education at NYU. Since I had already been accepted, I enrolled in the Engineering College, and started attending classes at the Manhattan campus. My memory isn't too clear whether I started as a day or night student, but I became a night student when I got a job as collection manager for The Mutual Finance Company in Mount Vernon. Once again, I made a favorable first impression, being hired out of so many applicants.

I had been away for four and a half years, and nothing was as it was. I had no buddies, my little black book of old girlfriends was totally outdated and useless, college classes were hard, and in the back of my mind was always the Bar in Trani. I always thought of it as my Bar, and felt a responsibility for it, especially because no money had ever been sent to my parents from the time it had opened. Actually, any letters from my uncle Amerigo stressed how tight things were, and that additional funds would be welcome. That wasn't going to happen! I had a few dates with girls, but nothing worthwhile. Those Italian girls had made quite an impression, and the American girls just didn't measure up. They seemed so shallow! I visited my old Army buddy Mike Danze in Brooklyn, and went out with his sister once, but she wasn't my type, although I wouldn't have been able to tell you what my type was. I exchanged a few letters with Hilda in Austria, but that wasn't going to go anywhere, and it soon stopped.

Mike asked me if I would coach him and his buddies play baseball. Having time on my hands, I agreed, and formed a little athletic club. Since it was still winter, we did other things, like basketball and running track. I would get them up early in the morning to run around the track at Mt. St. Michael. We had meetings and dues, and fun punishments, like Tommy Rumpf dressing in ladies clothing, and pushing a baby carriage with another guy in it, in front of St. Anthony's Church after Sunday Mass.

I also talked the police officer in charge, to let me have the keys to the PAL recreation room in Mt. Vernon. We had exclusive use of the facility, and held our weekly meetings there. It was a lot of fun, and by the time the baseball season came around, the kids were in really good shape, and I don't remember them losing any games in league play while I coached. Mike tells me that they still remember their "coach", and send regards when they speak to him.

Work was OK. As a collection manager, I was in charge of collecting delinquent accounts, and I don't think I had the right frame of mind for the job. Being always almost broke myself, I tended to sympathize with those people that were going through hard times. Sometimes, I was able to buy them additional time by making up stories. Other times I would make a payment of five dollars just so their account wouldn't be turned over to the attorney. One such case was of a young black couple, living in Public Housing in Mt. Vernon. He would get up every day, and stand on the corner with other day laborers, hoping to earn a day's pay. Sometimes he got lucky, most times not. He was a young guy, and didn't want to ruin his credit, but there's just so much he could do. One day I went to his apartment, and his wife let me in. She showed me the infant sitting in the high chair, and then opened the refrigerator for my inspection. It was empty except for half a small bowl of baked beans. She said, "Until my husband comes home, I don't know if my baby will have anything else to eat. If he did work today, do you think we should spend those few dollars on food, or pay you so that he can keep a good credit rating?" How could I tell her that their credit was already shot! I told her not to worry about it, and paid five dollars on the account.

Of course there were people on the other side that were not so honorable. One was a bookie that had gotten the maximum loan of $500, and then disappeared. I wound up tracking him to his new address, then following him to work, and then served his boss with a garnishee, whereby a percentage of his wages would be held back each week. I was very proud of my detective work, but only very briefly. He promptly quit his job, and we were back to square one, playing cat-and-mouse games. Fortunately, although connected to the local mob, he liked me, and I never felt that I was in danger. Maybe it was because we were both of Italian descent. After months of hassling, I asked him if he had any intention of ever paying back his debt. With a very serious face, he said "I give you my solemn oath, that if there ever comes a day that I'm caught out in the rain without an umbrella, and I have to duck into a doorway, and if that doorway happens to be the entrance to The Mutual Finance office, I'll come up and pay off the whole thing!" I knew then it was a lost cause for sure.

At home, my father was still working as a master bricklayer, meaning that he worked on bringing up the corners of the building, while others would work "on the line". He dictated the pace of the work, and was very valuable to the builders. So much so, that the foreman would pick him up personally every morning, and drive him to work. He was the first to be hired, and the last to be let go when the building was done. Every week, he could count on finding and extra 50-100 dollars in cash in his pay envelope. Plus, on rainy days when others would be sent home, he was paid full wages. He enjoyed bragging about being a "primadonna" in the business. He would have liked nothing more than to have me join him in the trade, but it wasn't for me. The work was too hard. He arranged to have me work on one of his jobs, and I lasted about a week. Of course, I wasn't trusted to lay bricks. I would work on the back-up walls that nobody saw, or lay cinder blocks with the other "donkeys". When time came for lunch, my father would come and get me to go off the work site. Sometimes, the shortest way was to walk across a plank connecting two walls of the building, many floors above the ground, with no safety net! My father walked the plank like it was Main Street, and he and his buddies found it funny when I froze. I don't know how I made it across once, but it was the first and last time. No sir, bricklaying was definitely not for me. A few years later, he tried again with Mike, with more success. Mike learned how to lay bricks well enough to consider a career of contracting home repairs on his own, but didn't want to follow in my father's footsteps. Actually, he wanted to study medicine, but we'll come to that later on.

Sometime in the spring of 1955, a classmate asked me to double date with him and his girlfriend for a night of bowling. A great idea, but I had no girlfriend. It was out on Long Island, so I thought it would be a good idea to ask Aida if she wanted to go. We visited them regularly, and I had even dated her best friend Carol Ritti briefly. Another one of those forks in the road! Mario was still in the service, and it seemed like a good idea. Well, it went OK, and we decided to go out again, and again, and soon were going steady. The parents were happy, and life was good. Of course, Mario was discharged about that time, and wasn't sure it was a good idea, mainly because he didn't want to see me get hurt, and possibly ruin our friendly family relationship.

However, he was also confused about what he was going to do with his own life, and we didn't see a whole lot of each other. It didn't matter though, because our bond had been forged, and we were best friends forever. He got a job as an Arthur Murray dance instructor, and it was tailor-made for him. No shortage of parties and girls, and his good looks only made it better. Not a bad way to pass the time until he decided what he was going to do with his life.

That summer we had the unique opportunity to vacation in Lake George. Mary Dammacco's oldest brother, Franco Mastromauro, had a house on the lake, and invited us up. What a fantastic experience! It was another window to look into a life far different from my own, and certainly something to strive for.

Franco Mastromauro had not gone back to Italy with his family, and had not participated in the Pastificio. He established his own successful business here. He had been an iceman, like my uncle Larry, but with a better business head. When he saw that the ice business had no future, he expanded to include coal deliveries. When he saw that it also was changing, he switched to fuel oil, and used his customers as a base for the Mastro Sunshine Fuel Oil Company. He did very well for himself. I'm guessing that the name "Sunshine" was a sentimental referral to their beginning in America, where the family had jobs at the Sunshine Biscuit factory in Jamaica.

While the others had sent money back to Italy regularly, so that Leonardo could fulfill his dreams for a Pastificio, Franco went it alone, and succeeded here. The Mastromauro and Dammacco families had been estranged for many years, primarily because Franco saw Mike Dammacco as a good-for-nothing, and had never approved of the marriage. They had worked together in the ice business, and had a falling out. Supposedly, Franco turned Mike in to the Immigration Authority as an illegal immigrant. Mike had to leave the country, and then reenter again. Sounds reasonable, because uncle Larry (who also entered illegally), did the same thing. Went up to Canada, and then reentered legally. Of course, each family had its own version.

Be that as it may, the Dammaccos of the fifties were not the Dammaccos of the thirties! They had returned from Italy with a share in the new Pastificio, and just had to sit tight while the earnings paid for their share. So, the families made up, and began to socialize. Franco's property on Lake George was actually an estate, supposedly formerly owned by a Countess. Besides the big house, it had a couple of smaller guesthouses, as well as a former stable. These were in disrepair, and not in use. There was a boathouse, but no boat. Nevertheless, it made a lasting impression. My mother, Mike, and I, went with Mary, Aida, Angela, and Maria up to Lake George. Franco's wife Lydia, and children "Booby" and Mary hosted us. The husbands came up on the weekend, as did Mario and his latest heartthrob Val, a really gorgeous girl. We had a really good time, and two incidents stand out. One was that while on the boardwalk outside the boathouse, I got the urge to push Aida into the water. We had our bathing suits on, and I thought it was funny. That's when I first realized that she wasn't a good sport. She did not take it well at all, considering that we were supposed to be boyfriend and girlfriend! The other was when we had rented a motorboat to go around on the lake, and visit some of the other towns. Getting back on the boat after one of these stops, Mike hesitated for a moment, with one foot on the edge of the boat, and the other on the dock. The hesitation caused the boat to pull away from the dock, and in slow motion, Mike did a spread-eagle, and then fell in the water. It was really very funny, and he's been kidded about it ever since. My cute little baby brother! He was intelligent, accomplished, determined, and lovable. It's just that he had a knack for occasionally doing things that were hilarious, and I never let him forget it. It was always clear to me that he was an exceptional individual, and have always loved him dearly.

## I get married

Sometime after that summer, I was forced to make a life-altering decision. I was out with the Dammacco family at a nightclub on Long Island, where the Italian singer Lou Monte (Peppino, the Italian Mouse) was appearing. Aida and I were on the dance floor, when she suddenly asked, "Where are we going with this?" For a second, I didn't have a clue what she was talking about. Then it hit me, as did the realization that her parents had probably put her up to it. I wasn't offended. It seemed like a perfectly legitimate question, considering that we had been "going steady" for a few months, and had known each other for years. I still had some reservations, but I was convinced that was because of the family influence. I was positive that given a chance to grow on her own, that Aida and I would become more compatible. The positives outweighed the negatives. She was a very pretty Italian-American girl, with the families from the same town, and I felt very comfortable with her.

All these things ran around my head in a matter of seconds, while we danced, and she was waiting for an answer. I tried to buy myself a little time by asking back, "Well, where do you want it to go?" It was lame, and I don't remember what she said back. It was clear that it was up to me! Well, I wouldn't have been there if I didn't want to be there. Besides, committing myself would resolve the question that had been in my mind since my teen-age years, "Who am I going to marry? What will she look like?" Well, the answer was in front of me, and it looked pretty good. So, we went back to the table, and announced that we were "going steady". Everybody was happy!

However, having pressed that button, I was now forced to evaluate my life, and make plans. I was working at the Mutual Finance Company days, and attending NYU Engineering nights. A degree was at least five years away, and there was a bar in Italy that wasn't doing us any good. If I was going to be an Engineer, then my time at Mutual Finance served only to earn a living. Even after getting a degree, it would take years to establish a career, and what would happen to the money invested in the bar?

It became clear that I had to address the problem with the bar before doing anything else. I don't remember the exact order of things, but I announced my intentions to the families. After some thought, the Dammaccos suggested it might be a good idea not to do anything until I came back from Italy. From their point of view, it seemed like a reasonable request, but it made no sense to me! I had no idea how long I would be gone, if I was going to be successful or not, and what would I do if it didn't work out? I didn't need the additional problem of being committed to someone and wondering if they would stay true while I was gone. I had seen too many guys get "Dear John" letters in the Army. Besides, I was young and healthy, and didn't know what temptations I might be subjected to. Nanni might still be available! Who knows? If not married, I wanted to be free!

They saw the value in my thinking, and everything else is a blur. The formal asking for Aida's hand in marriage, the engagement party, the wedding, the honeymoon, and the trip to Italy. Truth to tell, Mary Dammacco did all the organizing, and all I had to do was show up. My parents paid for half of the wedding expenses, because the Dammaccos didn't have enough money. Their income from the Pastificio was going directly to pay for their share, and they had to bide their time. Actually, we loaned them money from the cash we got at the wedding so that they could pay off the bills. We got married on January 21$^{st}$, 1956, and left for Italy in March.

With Mario, Angela, and Maria

A couple of notable experiences from this period that I can share are funny. Aida had a hard time adjusting to the idea that she was married, and had this compulsion to call her mother regularly during our honeymoon. Of course, she was grilled for the "earthy" details, and much of the time was spent giggling. Our honeymoon was spent at Strickland's in the Poconos, a honeymoon mill. Aida couldn't understand why so few people were out socializing in the afternoons.

After the honeymoon, we spent a couple of weeks at my house, and a couple of weeks at the Dammaccos. They let us use their master bedroom, but they didn't understand the concept of privacy! After we had gone to bed, Mary could pop in at any time, just to check that we were warm enough, or to tuck the blankets under a little better. One morning I woke up to find the whole Dammacco family, except for Mike, standing lined up along the walls, with big grins on their faces. Mary couldn't believe her daughter was married, Angela wanted to know how it felt to lay in bed with a man, Maria kept giggling, and I felt like a piece of meat in a showroom window. Even Mario got his digs in. I thought I had gotten used to them, but this was a bit much. Although, I had to admit, it was funny! In retrospect, they were the last carefree days of my life!

\* \* \*

## The Italian Stay – the personal experience

So much happened in our time in Italy, and it's too confused in my mind to try to tell everything at once. So, I'll break it into a personal and business side, and see if I can make it any easier.

We left for Italy on the Andrea Doria in March. Good thing! She sank a few months later (July 25, 1956). The trip was an extension of our honeymoon, and although I knew where we were going, I had no clue as to what I was going to do when I got there. The only thing that I knew for sure was that I had to evaluate things in terms of dollars, and compare it with what I could be earning in the States. The dollar was much stronger than the Lira, and I didn't want to waste years earning what I could in months back home. Other than that, I was ready for anything! Well, I thought I was!

In retrospect, the lack of fear in what I was undertaking is puzzling. We were a young couple, with no money, no home, in a foreign country, and an uncertain business. It couldn't be stupidity, so I can attribute it only to extreme self-confidence. Aida assumed I knew what I was doing, and I saw it as an adventure with a safety valve. If things didn't work out, I could always run back home.

It was a real pleasure to see my uncle Amerigo again. With his wife Adalgisa and sons Michele and Aldo, he was managing the bar on our behalf, and was always his lovable self. Everybody liked him. Our partner Gino Povia was his usual self, proud of his reputation, and determined to make a bigger name for himself. With his wife Maria, and children Anna and Franco and Piero, they became our family.

The first order of business was getting an apartment, for which I had done absolutely no preparation. I quickly found out there was an extreme shortage of suitable apartments, but zia Teresa came to the rescue. She was estranged from Giuseppe (Peppino) Mastromauro, but still had the apartment in the old Pastificio building in Corato, as did the other Mastromauros (mother, Nunzio, and Attilio). They all welcomed us warmly, and she told us to use her apartment until we got settled. It was beautifully furnished, and it made us feel like we were still on our honeymoon. It also had the advantage of being company for Aida, while I was gone all day. I commuted by bus to Trani, and didn't get home until late evening. Not a good life for a young married couple, but it was tougher on Aida than it was on me. Stuck alone all day, having to learn to cook from scratch (no supermarkets), no TV to speak of (two public black and white TV stations, which showed old movies, and went off the air around 11 PM).

The separation took its toll, but I was unable to find an apartment in Trani. Finally, we asked the widowed grandma Mastromauro if we could live in the Villino in

Trani. Nobody was using it, and we would occupy only the ground floor. She agreed, and we finally had a place of our own. Not only that, but it felt like we were coming home, because that's where the Dammaccos had lived when they were in Italy. I felt the same because I had spent so much time there. It was on Via Bisceglie, about a half mile outside of town, and it was a long walk to the bar, but it was worth it. The villa had two floors, was on a large piece of property that was planted with grapevines, surrounded by walls and a large gated entrance.

What it didn't have was furniture, hot water, a bathtub, or heat. I arranged to have our old bedroom furniture, which was stored in Corato, sent to Trani, but we didn't feel the full effect of the other things until winter. I would still classify this period as "adventurous". Aida would not! Having to wash clothes by hand in an outside tub, using a washboard and lie soap was totally foreign to her, and not something she was prepared for. Neither was the long walk into town to go shopping, and learning to cook! It was especially hard because there were no "things in a can" to make it easier. I'm sure she felt that the old pioneer women had it easier. Me? I really liked it, but I had a better life. I wasn't "stuck" there all day. That isn't to say I wasn't having problems, but that's the other side, and I'll do it later.

Little by little, we resolved the problems. We bought a Fiat 600 car, and that took care of the transportation. Aida accompanied Gino and Maria Povia on a business trip to a

Milan Fair, and purchased a dining room set. After delivery, Gino commissioned a glass covering for the dining room table, and the effect was striking. Furthermore, I installed a water heater and bathtub in the small room adjoining the bedroom. I tell you; that first bath with running hot water, in my own tub, was accompanied by a feeling of indescribable luxury!

That summer was a great summer! The Dammaccos came. First Angela and Maria. We drove to Rome to pick them up. Then Mike and Mary, now mom and dad. Even Mario managed to come for a couple of weeks. At the Bar, Gino had been asked by the town to operate the summer club and restaurant that it was opening at the spiaggia. It was called La Lampara. After he had hired all the personnel (maitre-de, chefs, waiters, bar-men, etc.), it was agreed that I would run the day-to-day operation there. It was great fun, and very satisfying for me to show a healthy profit at the end of the summer. In the meantime, I got to play Humphrey Bogart in Casablanca. Anybody who was anybody would come to the club to eat or dance, and I hosted. Everybody knew me from my previous life there, and fortunately, there were no incidents. My main function was to keep the chefs happy, so that they wouldn't start throwing knives at the waiters. Boy, are they a touchy bunch! The good ones see themselves as artists, and behave accordingly. Unfortunately, the maitre-de also sees himself in the same way, as do the really good waiters. It was a job to massage all those egos on a daily basis, and I think I did a great job. Had only one major problem! Trani had been chosen as the site for a national event called "Festival della Canzone", and we were hosting the dinner for the executives and cast after the performance. Two hundred fifty dinners plus! Stressful for everyone! As we were getting ready, the maitre-de asked the main chef to make him look good that evening! Major mistake! The main chef quit on the spot, and walked out! They came running to me, and I went running after the chef! I caught up to him, walking on the road back to town, and eventually was able to turn him around and come back to work! Whew! That was one close call.

While I'm on the subject, I should tell you how much I came to admire and appreciate those good cooks and waiters. By the end of the summer, I did come to see them as artists. A good chef orders well, makes good use of everything in the kitchen, keeps waste to a minimum, and is primarily responsible for the image that people walk away with. I watched him take a cooked pheasant, skin it, cut it into bite-sized pieces, and then reassemble it as if it hadn't been touched. A good waiter makes people think that they are the only ones being served, and is at his best when conditions are at their worst, like overcrowding or late food. A maitre-de is like a conductor, who sets the harmony for the place. He can also be worth his weight in gold, steering diners to more expensive dinners and wines, especially evaluating how much the people can afford. Our maitre-de was especially good. One of the first things he insisted on was an "antipasto cart". He dressed the shelves with mouthwatering delicacies. Then, when people were ready to order, he would roll up the cart, and ask if they would prefer a "custom" antipasto. It never failed, especially if a guy was trying to impress the girl. The antipasto would cost more than the dinner!

Another little trick he did at the bar. He put a leather cup on the bar, with five dice in it, from 10's to aces. The bartender then encouraged people to play poker, rather than argue to see who would pay for the drinks. This also encouraged the loser to want to try it again! You might say that he was a con man. I would say that he was a real artist!

You would imagine that I would take advantage of this great cuisine, and you would be right. I had a table set up for our family, and we had our dinner in the afternoon. It was also designed to impress my just-arrived in-laws, and it did! This was a good time, because most of our activity was at night, and I could relax and enjoy during the day. That is, after all the shopping and preparations had been completed.

In the morning, I would get together with the master chef, to plan the menu for that evening. It depended on what was available in the walk-in refrigerator, or any leftovers from the previous day, and what the chef thought would be good entrees. I might make a suggestion or two, but he had the final say. Then he would prepare a shopping list for me. I established relations with different butchers and produce men, to ensure that I got the best that was available on the market. I must have done a good job, because the chefs never complained of the quality of what I brought back. Along the way, I picked up a few tricks. For example, the chef told me about a cut of meat that could be passed off as filet mignon, but was much less expensive. Even the butchers were surprised that I had such "inside" information. While I'm at it, I should say a few words about the waiters, and their expertise. Besides following up on the maitre-de's lead, their job was to relieve the diners of as much money as possible. Since this was before the advent of credit cards, getting a feel of how much money the diners were carrying was an art form. It was comprised of good listening skills, calculated conversations, and sincere suggestions. Of course, impeccable service and great food were a given, as were the band and the atmosphere. The waiters competed with each other, and made sure to register a particularly good "score" with the maitre-de and myself.

No, there was no sense of guilt on my part. This was not a family restaurant, and although more expensive, people were getting their money's worth, and leaving happy. Besides, almost all our clientele were known wealthy residents. We never took advantage of the exceptions. Nevertheless, watching my people operate was a pleasure. It was like watching a band of great pickpockets, much like Fagin in "Oliver Twist".

La Lampara was an open-air club overlooking the beach, and the view was great! Well, believe it or not, after about two weeks of fine dining, I couldn't take it any more. Everything started to taste the same, and the view was just a view, so we went back to home cooking. I still remember how much I enjoyed that first plate of pasta and piselli (peas).

The nightlife was something else. Live music and dancing. Invariably, the family would dress up, and hang out at La Lampara. Mario would pick somebody up, and ask to borrow my car for a while. I kidded him that he was ruining the springs on my car, with all the bouncing that he was doing in it. He swore that everybody was picking <u>him</u> up, so I put him to the test. I told him to just stand there, and not say a word to anyone, just to prove him wrong. Son-of-a-gun! Within minutes, a good-looking woman comes up, and asks if he's an American. He says yes, but doesn't encourage her. Finally, she decides to leave, but gives Mario her business card, and asks him to call her when he gets back home. Now, I'm a believer! Mom and dad Dammacco were good dancers, and especially liked to dance the tango. Mario was also very good due to his Arthur Murray days, and Aida preferred to dance with him rather than me, with good reason.

All good things come to an end, and so did the summer. I should mention that everything that we consumed at La Lampara was charged to my account. It wouldn't have been fair to Gino otherwise. To his credit, when we were going over the numbers after the season, he told the bookkeeper to treat my charges as a business expense. I like to believe it was because I had earned it, showing a handsome profit, and not once asking for his help.

Before closing the chapter on the summer, I should record an unpleasant experience. The Mastromauros, never wanting for internal family squabbling, added one that was exceptional, even for them! During the summer, Frank Mastro, the oldest brother, made a surprise visit, saying that he wanted to see the whole family again, and there was much happiness at the occasion. The brothers hadn't seen each other in a long time, although the Dammaccos had been seeing him regularly, and were very chummy. He was welcomed like the lost sheep, and a good time was had by all! Well, at least for a few days! One morning, he showed up at the villa, saying that he needed to speak to his sister urgently. He went over the old days with her, cried at some of the things that had been done, and wanted her input on many things. It went on for a couple of hours! Eventually, he got to the reason for his coming to Italy. It seems he felt that he had been unfairly denied a share of the new Pastificio, and was laying claim to it. Unspoken was his question, that if Mary could have a share, why not him? What he didn't say was that he had recorded the whole conversation (the recorder was in his briefcase)! Who knows what he had gotten her to say? Anyway, armed with his new weapon, he went back to his brothers. He challenged them to give him a share or he would sue!

Actually, Mary had never been "given" a share. She had to pay for that share out of the Pastificio earnings. Frank didn't want to pay anything! Eventually, the brothers bought him off, but he was such a dirtbag! Funny thing happened one day during the mess. I was driving Mike (my father-in-law now) to Corato, when we saw a Pastificio truck coming the other way. I don't know why, but Mike signaled for them to stop, and got out to take a look. Sure enough, Frank was sitting in the cab, hitching a ride to Trani. Mike was furious. He tried to pull Frank out, and was going to kick his ass, but I held him back. He then ordered the drivers to leave Frank on the road, and go about their business. He was the boss, so they agreed. That way, I was able to get Mike back in the car and continue on to Corato. In the rear-view mirror, I saw the truck turn around, and come back to pick up Frank. You must understand that all the workers liked Mike. They saw him as one of them, a worker. They also saw how badly the brothers-in-law treated him, and how they showed him no respect. They also knew that Frank, no matter how bad he might be, was still a Mastromauro, and the brothers would still prefer him to Mike. Fortunately, Mike was looking forward, and still fuming, so he didn't see it.

I said the brothers (Nunzio, Peppino, and Attilio) bought him off, but how they did it should be noted. They never wanted the sister as a partner, and but for the insistence of the father Leonardo, she wouldn't have been one. So, they bought Frank off for $10,000. He had his own big business, and didn't need the Pastificio. Just wanted to break chops, and get something for nothing. He certainly didn't want to spend years and money fighting in the Courts. After Frank signed off, the brothers turned on their sister, and insisted that she pay the full amount of the payoff! After all, it was all her fault that Frank got agitated, and she got herself tape-recorded with damaging information! They even felt that she should be so thankful to them, for rescuing her from such a terrible situation! She agreed, and the amount was added to her debt. What a family!

The summer over, the Dammaccos returned home, and the winter was cold and lonely. Fortunately, the DeToma family became like an extended family, and we spent quite a bit of time with them and all their kids. They had given Aida a gorgeous gold necklace as a wedding gift, and treated us as their own. Mrs. DeToma got a special kick out of seeing us coping with our life, and was impressed with Aida's neatness! She would think nothing of coming to the villino, unannounced, with some of her friends, and then proceed to open all the drawers for all to see! She just couldn't believe how neat and orderly everything was, and would pull these sneak attacks to test her! She would then turn to her friends and say, "See? Didn't I tell you?" She was always surprised, but so proud of Aida, as if she was her own daughter. Of course Franco was still my best buddy, but he was single, and I had responsibilities.

Aida's strong suite was cleaning. Cooking was a whole other world. At home, that had been Angela's responsibility. So, a little at a time, she ventured into the new world. I just made sure not to criticize, and eat everything with gusto, especially the failures! Eventually, she got a handle on it, and life was good. Some things she just couldn't handle, like fish! Didn't like to touch it. Occasionally, she would give it a try, but always had to give up. We kidded her, especially the time that a calamari got stuck in the drain, and she wouldn't put her finger in there to pry it out, but she really tried. She even bottled tomato sauce for the winter! Actually, Maria Povia asked her if she wanted to learn how to do it. What a job! Boil cases of tomatoes, "pop" the skins, fill the jars, and place them in boiling water to make a vacuum. Place a basil leaf on top, and tighten the lid. Then wait for the jars to cool slowly, and store away. It was a sight to see them at work in the back of the bar, and the adjoining sidewalk. If the girls from Middle Village could only have seen her! It lasted us the whole winter, and we've never had a tastier sauce.

As I said, it was a long and cold winter. No TV, and no heat. I bought a gas heater, but it was only good within five feet of where we placed it. The villino rooms were too large for just that one heater, and it became our best friend. Near the table when we ate, sitting around it when relaxing, moving it into the bedroom for the night. Of course, we had to remember to always have a pot of water nearby, for humidity. Otherwise, our throats would go dry. We thought it was dangerous to leave it on while we slept, so we shut it off for the night. Of course, in the morning, we didn't want to leave the warm covers to start it up again. Of course, I was the man, so it was my job!

Going to bed was also an ordeal. The sheets were so cold! We would pass a hot iron over the spot we expected to lay on, and then cuddled under the blankets, sharing our body heat and a hot water bottle. I don't know how long we stayed without moving, waiting to warm up. Any move was a reminder of how cold the rest of the bed was, in spite of full flannel pajamas. Eventually, we'd drift off, and awoke in a nice warm bed. What a hero I was, to volunteer to leave it, and face another cold day!

Eventually, we got through to the spring. We socialized with the Povias, the DeTomas, as well as some from the old crowd. We managed to take a nine-day vacation, driving up into Germany and Austria, visiting Salzburg, Berchesgarten, and Mondsee, my old Army stomping grounds. What was so fantastic was that we did it with no money! Well, that's an exaggeration, but we really had very little money, and were amazed at the time at how much we got to do. Aida remembers not being able to afford to buy a loaf of black bread from Germany before returning. She would remember that!

In addition, I was talked into playing basketball again (it didn't take much convincing). We traveled to Caserta, and a couple of other towns. Didn't win the championship, but had fun. My condition for playing was that Aida had to come on our trips, since I was now a serious married man. They paid for our own separate room, but always had trouble when checking in with the team at the hotels. We had to show our passports to prove that we were married.

Summer of '57 came, and those cold winter nights caught up to us! Aida was pregnant, and expected in September. We wanted a good doctor, and were recommended to go to a private clinic in Bari, called Villa Bianca. Doctor Pesce had been trained in The States, but had never heard of "painless childbirth"! Called it nonsense, "Fesserie Americane"! So, we drove to Bari weekly for classes, together with Nicola Menga and his wife, who was also expecting. He owned the largest marble processing plant in Trani, of which there were many. Aida learned breathing exercises to control the pain, and I was amazed at the movies showing what a woman goes through during childbirth! The contortions of the spinal column, so that the baby can come out! The only thing that I could compare it to, was Lon Chaney turning into the wolfman! WOW!

Aida carried very well, and had never been prettier. She actually shone! The added weight agreed with her, but she carried the baby totally up front. From the back she looked normal. She insisted on swimming, and it was quite a sight to see her paddling on her back, with this huge belly up in the air. It looked like a floating island! The Dammaccos came again, and they were invaluable. Mom did all the work, and Aida was able to get her rest. Mario even came, and we were all there at the Villa Bianca when Marco was born in the early morning of September 22nd, 1957. Mario left the same day, but he was the godfather.

All those lessons to have a pain-free childbirth went out the window with the first contraction! They only served to give us an early warning, so we could drive from Trani to Bari, with Aida letting the world know of each and every contraction. By the time we got her settled in the bed at the hospital, I was swearing that I would never ever put her through such pain ever ever again! She was in labor for about three hours (it seemed like three weeks), until she had dropped enough to take her into the delivery room. We weren't allowed in, but could hear the screaming from the other side of the door! Those poor doctors! She must have gotten one of them pretty good, because we later saw marks on her wrists, showing that she had obviously been restrained!

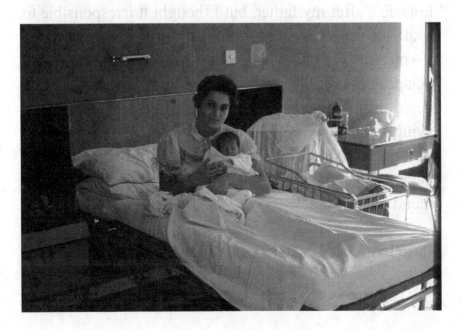

Marco was hairy and beautiful, and within the week, we were back at the villino. Thank God for mom and dad Dammacco. They took care of everything, and Aida was able to rest and get adjusted to the idea of being a mother, and what a monumental responsibility it was. There were some beautiful moments, such as Aida breastfeeding, the baby sleeping, the baby awake, the baby crying, the baby being bathed, etc. You get the picture. My favorite was watching the grandparents give Marco a bath. While mom bathed and dried him, dad would make sure the gas heater was close enough to get maximum heat. He would also pre-heat the diapers before they touched the baby's skin, and would shield the overhead light bulb, so that light wouldn't shine directly into the baby's eyes.

Why did we choose "Marco" as a name? It should have been "Ignazio", after my father, but I thought it irresponsible to saddle an innocent child with such an uncommon name in America. I remembered what I had gone through with "Sciancalepore". Also, we wanted a name that wouldn't be altered or abbreviated. We had gone to a movie in Trani, having to do with the Roman Empire, and Marcus Aurelius. We thought "Marco" was perfect! Italian; Strong; Proud; Uncommon, but not unique. We added "Ignazio" as a second name.

Mario left for the States right after Marco was born.

A few weeks later, I left for the States as well! Aida and the baby stayed behind. They were in good hands until I got settled. Once again, I was broke!

## The Italian Stay – the business experience

As I said before, I had no specific plan as to what I was going to do when I got to Italy, other than evaluate the earning possibilities. Knowing that I could return to the States was a great safety cushion on which to rely on. In the back of my mind, I knew that the bar would have to earn quite a bit of money to offset my potential earning power back home. Considering the fact that we had not received a penny in the years that the bar had been operating, the prospect didn't seem too promising. I had visited a couple times while I was in the service in Austria, but that was more of a vacation, and I never had gotten into the nitty-gritty of the business.

It was immediately clear that money was tight. Business and personal expenses were always considered on a priority basis. That is to say, there wasn't enough cash to pay all bills when due. So, payments were put off as much as possible, especially when money was needed for personal expenses. That's how we managed to get a car, a dining room set, a bathtub and water heater, a vacation, etc. Actually, when Aida walked into town to go shopping, she would stop by the bar first to get money. I took money out of the register for my daily expenses, and Gino and I would also take out cash for personal expenses on an irregular basis. Considering that uncle Amerigo's salary came out of my share, my finances became even more strained.

It was also clear that the problem wasn't traffic. The Bar Centrale, or Bar Povia, was the go-to place in Trani. It was in the center of town, and the pastry was of the best quality. It was a splendid place to sit and people watch. Furthermore, we catered weddings and other occasions. Gino's reputation had become regional, and people came from the surrounding towns to book our services. We were considered the best in the business. I was very proud to be connected with such a business.

We also furnished smaller bars in town with pastries on a daily basis. Uncle Amerigo made the rounds in a station wagon that Gino had bought for that purpose, as well as to bring supplies and personnel to our catering locations. In addition to operating the restaurant La Lampara during the summer, we also operated the bar in the private club "Circolo dei Signori" in Trani, which also contributed to additional catering business. Of course, more business was welcome, but we had a pretty good flow. Sometimes, especially preparing for Feast days and catering at the same time, we ran out of space to put all the goods being prepared. These were times when we worked 24 to 48 hours straight. It was a sight to see everybody dragging at the end of such a period. I remember one time, Gino was so tired that he didn't have the strength to go back home, so he went behind some stacks of paper products and fell asleep on the floor. While he lay there, a new customer came in the back, wanting to place an order for a future catering. The head baker, also very tired himself, patiently took the order and escorted the customer out. Gino was not seen sleeping, and fortunately, he didn't snore. It was something we laughed about later when the confusion was over, and we were more rested.

We would regularly sit with the accountant, and review the numbers and the reasons for our difficulties. The results were always the same. The overhead was too high. Although the pastry making and the catering operations were profitable, the bar portion of the operation was a loser. We justified this by saying that the bar was promoting the pastry business, and that the loss was the cost of the promotion. We tried to think of alternate uses for the two rooms adjoining the bar, but couldn't think of anything that didn't require an additional investment. In the winter, people would sit in there, and we had table service, but it wasn't enough to offset the cost. There was nothing we could do about the rent. As a matter-of-fact, there was always the threat of an increase.

Gino and I got along very well, but there was one cause for some friction. I believed that Gino was pricing too low. While this was justified in the early years, the name was now established, and I felt we could charge more. Gino hated to turn away business, and would lower the prices to close a deal. To compound the problem, after the catering had been done, people insisted on an additional discount from the balance remaining. This was not much of a problem with the average people, that is, the working people. They were respectful, thankful, and even tipped extra for the excellent service. The problem was with the professionals. The judges, attorneys, professors, teachers, etc. They demanded top service, but wanted discounted prices. Plus, we had to chase them for the balance, and then they would ask for an additional discount on that balance. Not all of them, but most of them. Although Gino agreed to charge more, he never did. Getting his name known was his primary goal, not making a good profit. Consequently, the profit was not enough to pay the overhead, and the noose began to tighten.

What was I doing to contribute to the operation? Well, in hindsight, if I had devoted my time to learning the pastry business, I would have at least learned a trade. I chose instead to follow the money, so I sat at the cash register. I also opened the bar at 6:00AM, and made espressos until the regular barman arrived at eight. I interacted with the customers, and helped create a happy atmosphere in the front, while the serious business was being done in the back.

I went along on some of the catering operations, supposedly to make sure that everything went well. In reality, it was best that I stay out of the way when I did go. Reason being that Carlo and Giovanni, the two headwaiters, were truly professional, and I was constantly amazed at how efficiently they worked. During one of those wedding receptions, in a hall adjoining a movie theater, I made my contribution. During a break, I took most of the staff next door to the movie house. Up on the stage, I got us all to imitate The Rockettes! It was a poor imitation.

Besides, being a baker was very hard work, and I wasn't ready for that yet. To be fair, I really didn't see my future as a baker. I was there to make money, or else come back home, and resume my engineering studies. That first summer, I ran La Lampara, and showed a healthy profit at the end. I had come a long way from the kid in 1950, but I had no power other than that of persuasion.

As time passed, the financial situation became tighter. I would have a sleepless night, and wake up in the morning knowing that we had to pay the bank for some bills that day, or go into default. This came about because our credit had deteriorated, and some suppliers would not ship unless we signed a personal note to guarantee payment. So, if that note was not paid when due, the bank would send it to the "Notaio", who would certify the non-payment, and notify the police to padlock the business and proceed to satisfy that debt in whatever way he could.

The bank directors were our customers, as were the "Notaios", and they helped by "losing" the note for an extra day or two, but eventually, they even had had enough. A few times I was banging on the Notaio's office door after he had closed, so that I could give him the cash to satisfy a bill. We would have been scrambling all day, calling people that owed us money, sending Carlo out to collect on others, just so we could get cash to the Notaio before he closed. It was very belittling and embarrassing. The one that sticks out in my mind the most was how I took advantage of our local supplier of fresh eggs. Vincenzo was about my age, and his father had the fruit stand in the town market place. They were hard working people, and supplied us with the fresh eggs that we used to make the custards. It was usually cash on delivery, but as cash became more important to pay the bank, I got Vincenzo and his father to give us some temporary credit. The temporary became more permanent, and the amount kept increasing. He threatened to stop delivering, and I told him that then I would be forced to take the cash that we owed them to pay a new supplier. A lousy thing to do, but we didn't have any personal notes signed with them. I still remember the look on the kid's face; A mixture of anger, loathing, distrust, and helplessness. He continued supplying a little longer, until they realized that it was a lost cause. It's a very disturbing memory for me. Gino was also very concerned, and was always wheeling and dealing to make ends meet. As a matter of fact, there came a time that the debts started limiting what we could produce.

## Making the hardest decision of my life

Now, I can think of things that we could have tried, but at the time, all that I could see was that there was not enough cash to live on. For me, it was compounded by the fact that uncle Amerigo's salary was coming out of our share of the profits. I tried not to think about it, but there was no denying that it was a big problem. I loved him dearly, but something had to be done. When I finally was able to accept the fact that we might have to let him go, I started thinking of a compensation package to offer him. So, I went to the books, to review what he had been earning. You can't imagine my surprise!

On his last job as a chauffer, he had been earning 60K Lire a month. My mother had established his salary at 100K Lire, a healthy increase in salary, as well as position. That salary was more than what his brother Gennaro was earning, and Gennaro was an accountant. So, I was totally shocked to see that my uncle Amerigo had slowly increased his salary, and that over the last few years, he had averaged a little over 220K Lire a month! Since the draw was even for both partners, it was clear that my uncle had been taking the money that he should have been sending to his sister!

That took away any thoughts of severance compensation, but I still had to face the fact that I had to fire my uncle, the idol of my life, and who I loved very dearly. I kept putting it off and putting it off, but I suppose he felt it in the air. Fortunately, I caught a break. His wife Adalgisa was an elementary schoolteacher, and she had been on a waiting list for a position for many years. Amazingly, a position opened, and she was called, but it was back in the hometown of Corato. At the same time, her widowed aunt offered them her apartment in Corato, to live in rent-free. My uncle saw the handwriting on the wall in Trani, and he advised me that he was going to take advantage of the offers, and move back to Corato. How great! I didn't have to review any painful subjects, and we parted amicably. I never shared the discovery with my mother.

Left: Older brother Uncle Gennaro, wife
Anna, Adalgisa, uncle Amerigo
Right: Aldo, uncle Amerigo, Michele, aunt Adalgisa.

Apparently, uncle Amerigo had been able to put some money aside. After getting settled in Corato, and his wife working, he rented a small location, and opened up his own bar. Nothing fancy, serving mainly espresso coffee, but it gave him an additional income, and the opportunity to gab with people all day, which had always been his strong suite. I would see him a couple of times a week, bringing pastries, as I made my rounds of the other bars. His children Aldo and Michele were usually with him, since Adalgisa was working. Years later, after my uncle had passed away at an early age, I had occasion to visit aunt Adalgisa at her apartment. She told me that things had gone well with her and the children, but that she missed Amerigo's smiling face every day. I knew the feeling. The older son Michele had gotten a scholarship, and the younger one was very music oriented and bright. All I could think of was what a shame to lose a father at such a young age. I will always remember my uncle Amerigo fondly.

## A chance to salvage from a disaster

As we approached the summer of 1957, things were getting financially tighter and tighter. We started to fall behind on the rent payments, so as to pay those notes that seemed to show up every day. We really didn't have a plan. Fortunately, someone else did!

Pasquale DeToma, Franco's father, had a thought. Since we socialized quite a bit, he was aware of our situation. He thought the time was right to box and sell "paste secche" on a large scale. An outfit in one of the local towns had started doing that, and had grown quite a bit in a couple of years. He had a building that was empty. On the large property on Via Colonna where we had first met, was their summer home. Also on that property was a large unfinished villa. He had been building his dream home, when he wound up in an argument with his family in Brescia, and had to defend himself in the courts. So, construction had been stopped for the last seven years, but the underground area was complete. He proposed a partnership of three equal parts to launch the pastry industry. We had no money, so he accepted whatever equipment we had, together with our pots and pans, as our share of the partnership. He finished off the very large working area, including the latest baking oven, and a number of marble-top counters for work. When Gino said that he would make and package Panettoni, Pasquale had a special room built to Gino's specifications, to process the dough. He also bought a new station wagon, and had it printed with the company name. The existing company that I mentioned before was called IDEA. Industria Dolciaria e Affini. Pasquale wanted to have a sound-alike name, to take advantage of the existing Company. He came up with IDIA, Industria Dolciaria Italo-Americana.

What-the-Hell. The guy was even putting up the cash to buy the flour, sugar, and all else that was needed to get going. He should have a major say. We brought the baker and helpers, in addition to Gino's expertise. The understanding was very clear that Gino had the final say on everything that had to do with the product and production.

Gino went along with the whole plan, but it was clear that his heart wasn't in it. Although he never said it, I'm sure that he would have been much more motivated had we chosen his name for the new industry. Strangely, it was never discussed. I didn't want it because I didn't want to be committed to him, as I had been in the past. I think DeToma, being the crafty businessman that he was, felt the same way. Gino was being given the opportunity to use his trade to jump from being a good baker, to an industrialist.

Gino saw the possibilities, but wanted it on his terms, which was that he had to control everything. That wasn't going to happen! His role was to develop the products, and had final say in that area, but all other aspects had to be discussed and approved in council with the other partners. The idea was to relieve Gino of the office and distribution pressures, so that he could concentrate on making the most of his knowledge of pastry baking, of which he was a master. I handled the office, and got the goods needed for production that Gino requested, and Pasquale provided the money whenever needed. It seemed like an ideal arrangement, but it didn't work.

We quickly found out that the world wasn't waiting for our product. The salesman was having difficulty selling, because our price was higher than our competitor IDEA. The quality was far superior, but they wanted it at a lower price than the competition. These were obviously the growing pains of a new company, and I saw that we weren't going to be an overnight success, but it was a good idea, and there was room for us in the business. Unfortunately, my partners didn't see it the same way. DeToma had expected a quick return, and wasn't prepared to lay out an unlimited amount of money. Gino didn't want to produce a lower cost product, so that we could undersell IDEA. He considered it garbage, and would have nothing to do with it. I agreed with him, but pointed out that he then had to come up with something that IDEA didn't have, such as amaretti or the panettone. However, as I said before, his heart wasn't in the business, and he was doing less and less. He never baked a single panettone! At the time, the national companies Motta and Alemagna were producing the only panettoni on the market. Now everybody makes them, but then, we would have been one of the first. We missed a golden opportunity.

Gino started spending more time at the bar, leaving the bakers unsupervised. Pasquale contacted a couple of his wine wholesalers to handle the sales of the paste secche, and I would load up the van and make the deliveries to them down in Taranto and Lecce. The roundtrip took a whole day. One time, the weather was very bad, and I got back very late at night. The electricity had been knocked out in Trani, and when I got back home to the villino, I found that Aida had been sitting in the dark for hours, waiting for me. Life was tougher on her than it was on me, except for when her parents visited.

Unsupervised, there was no direction for the bakers. Plus, they saw the tension among the partners. They liked me, but their sympathies were with Gino, whom they considered to be a worker like themselves. I would always be l'Americano, and Pasquale DeToma was a rich man. Even so, one of the kids told me that there was some sabotage going on, and led me to where a large batch of expensive chocolate supplies had been buried in the ground outside the plant. I went into town to the bar, and tried to get Gino to understand that this was a major chance for us, and it couldn't be done without him. His major point was, "Why should I do all the work, and have to divide the profit three ways, when I can work for myself, and not share with anyone".

He never understood the concept, and remained just a small-time baker his whole life. We lost the bar after not paying the rent for a number of months. Gino rented an empty store, from which he baked pastries for local bars. Eventually, he moved to Verona, and opened a bar and pastry shop near the main square with the opera house. Many years later, together with my family and grown children, we visited him in Verona. We talked about the old times, but never of the bad stuff. His children had become bakers, and they all lived from the income of the bar. He owned his apartment and he and Maria were happy with their lives. We remained friends, and I never chided him for what he could have been.

IDIA was shut down, and there was nothing left for us there. Amazingly, the Italian experience had taken just a year and a half, but it seemed a lifetime. Actually, it had been a lifetime, and it was now time to return to my other life in America, and see where that would take me. Unfortunately, I was not returning as a conquering hero, but as a penniless failure.

Two weeks after Marco was born on September 22nd 1957, I left Aida in the care of her parents, and returned home.

## A new life, and the biggest loss of my life

I arrived home, but couldn't share the details of my Italian stay, other than that it was a failure, and that my parents had lost their money. How could I make them understand the details, and I certainly didn't want to tell my mother that her brother had not lived within his means. The bottom line was that they had lost the money, and my father harped on it every day to anyone who would listen, friend or stranger alike. Unspoken was the accusation that it was my mother's fault, since it had been her decision to make the investment. My father kept reminding everyone that he could have used the money to buy his own house. Instead, he was forced to live and pay rent in his brother's house. He was a workingman, and took the loss very hard. It was not a good atmosphere to live in, and my mother had been living in it for years. I felt so sorry that I had failed her.

1956

My brother was now nineteen years old. He had graduated from Cardinal Hayes in 1957, and was in his second year at NYU, studying pre-med. What a good kid. He was everything that I hadn't been; Studious, obedient, caring, dependable, and fun loving (this we had in common). He was a joy for our parents, and a great kid brother. Unlike me, he had made the most of his time at Cardinal Hayes. Like me, he had joined the band. Unlike me, he had actually learned to play an instrument (the saxophone) well. So much so that he had been on the school's swing band. He then had started his own band, The Jesters, with his neighborhood buddies, and they practiced in the garage at home. He was hip, with the haircut of the time called a d.a.(for duck's ass). This called for the longer sides to be slicked back, like a duck's feathers. He was hired to play at private dances. I went to watch him once, and it was hard to believe. There was my baby brother, up on a stage, leading a band and playing the sax. The music was good, it had a good beat, and kids were actually dancing to it. More than that, a bunch of girls were hanging out at the stage, clapping to the beat, and having a great old time. Mikey was a rock star! He also had a car (convertible), and had rigged a curtain that he could draw across the back window. It was red, with yellow initials (Cardinal Hayes' colors), and intended to be used in case he got some action in the back seat of the car. I don't know if he ever used that curtain. As I said, he was a really good kid. Of course, someday he may read this, and may want to fill in some details in self-defense. I will happily insert it here when he does.

Also unlike me, he didn't wait to get drafted. He joined the Air Force Reserves, thereby bypassing the draft, in exchange for a couple of months basic training, and a few years of occasional duty. It was a very smart move. He was no longer going with Geraldine (Gerry) Gelardo, the girl from when I had gotten married, where they had been usher and bridesmaid. He was free to play the field. Now, one would think that with all that was going for him, he would have had an attitude. Not so. He was still the nice kid he had always been. Unfortunately, the eight-year difference was still there, and we didn't have much in common. However, we really liked each other.

Thanks to the G.I. Bill, I resumed my Engineering studies at NYU, and it was a kick to go to school with Mike. We'd drive together to the University Heights campus in the Bronx, and he would go his way, and I mine. Occasionally we'd cross paths in study hall during the day, and it was clear we were in different generations. He was hanging out with his frat brothers, doing what college kids do, laughing and joking, planning their next party, etc. I was sitting with a bunch of exchange students from different European countries, all seriously studying, and preparing for the next class. Mike found this very funny, and I could see why.

Uncle Larry made me an offer that resolved all my problems. He wanted me to mind his bar on the weekend nights (Friday, Saturday, and Sunday), for which he would pay me $100 cash, and off the books. This would have been a great weekly salary for full-time job, and I was very appreciative. Not only did the income allow me to continue my studies as a full-time student, but also Aida and Marco could come join me; especially since my parents offered to let us use the parlor, formerly Mike's and my bedroom, as our bedroom. They took the smaller room, and Mike was set up with a bedroom in the attic. Everything fell into place, and Aida and Marco arrived between Christmas and New Years. Life was good and on track. I was going to make up for the lost time in Italy, and have an Engineering career in a few years.

Then, just like that, everything went to Hell, and so quickly! In five months my life would be turned upside down, and I would lose the anchor of that life. My mother had always been healthy, and took proper care of herself. She saw Dr.

Cerrato when necessary, and went to see a specialist for a yearly checkup. Shortly after the New Year, she was on the way to see the specialist, Dr. Baddia, in the city. She came back unexpectedly early; seems that while on the train to go downtown, her nose started to bleed. Holding a handkerchief to her nose, she made her way back home, and then to Dr. Cerrato. He gave her a physical examination, took blood, and sent it away for analysis. He had no clear idea of what it might be, but didn't think it was serious. When the results came back, we knew different! It was diagnosed as Leukemia. This was new to us, and Dr. Cerrato gave us a quick education. It was a very serious disease, and there were many strains of it, but there was hope that with the right medication, it could be controlled, and possibly put in remission. There were such cases, and we put our hopes on that. There followed a series of more detailed tests, the most painful of which was to get a sample of the marrow. This confirmed that not enough healthy cells were being formed, and that this was indeed a very serious situation.

My mother took all of this in stride, with her usual calmness, and continued to go about her daily chores as usual; taking her medications and going for treatments. This all helped us believe that it would turn out OK, or at least controlled. We were not at all prepared for the quick deterioration. She started losing her strength, to the point that after a few weeks, she became bedridden. Shortly thereafter, it was obvious that she needed to be hospitalized, and Dr. Cerrato made the arrangements for her to be admitted to

Westchester Square Hospital. That day is still memorable to me. There was no ambulance, and she wasn't strong enough to go down the stairs by herself. So, we sat her on a kitchen chair, and Mike and I carried her down the stairs, one step at a time. At the bottom, before going out the door, she forced herself to stand and told us, "Non facciamo scenate". Let's not make a scene! She didn't want to be seen carried in that condition. So, holding on to us on both sides, we made our way down the outside steps, and to the car. She was a firm believer in proper behavior, and a class act all the way.

Westchester Square Hospital wasn't specialized in her sickness, and Dr. Cerrato suggested that we transfer her to St. Vincent's Hospital in the city. They were doing experimental work on Leukemia, and she would have a better chance there. She was transferred, and we went to see her every day. After about two weeks, she asked me to take her out of there. St. Vincent's was also a teaching hospital, and she told me that there were always doctors in her room, discussing her case. Worse, they were always coming to take blood from her, day and night, and to prove the point, she showed me the inside of her arms. They were both black and blue, from top to bottom, from the needles used to take the blood samples. She wasn't getting any better, and was demoralized. I talked it over with Dr. Cerrato, accepted the inevitable, and he made the arrangements to have her transferred back to Westchester Square Hospital. There, her condition continued to deteriorate, but she persevered.

She consoled us during our visits, and we kept hoping for the best. She even asked to see Marco again. Since children weren't allowed in the room in those days, Aida stood with Marco in her arms, down in the street below the window in her room, which I think was on the second floor. She forced herself to go to the window and wave down.

Dr. Cerrato gave it one last try, and arranged for a consultation with a reputed Leukemia specialist from out of town. He came, visited with her, reviewed the charts, confirmed that there was nothing to be done, and that her time was short. There was nothing left to do but wait for the inevitable, and we took turns staying with her, and making conversation. She never despaired, never complained, and never acknowledged that she was dying. She went into a coma, and I felt I had missed the chance to tell her how much I loved her, what a wonderful person she was, and how much she meant to me. Being alone in the room with her, I sat by her bed, held her hand, and told her all of that, plus apologizing for being such a lousy son, and for failing her trust in me.

I swear, I felt her squeeze my hand!

A little later, while I had fallen asleep in the chair, she took her last breath. The nurses awoke me to tell me the news, and they were all tearing! These women, to whom death is a daily occurrence, are hardened to the experience. However, having come to know my mother, they also felt the loss of an exceptional person. She died in the early morning of Friday, May 9th, 1958. <u>Sunday would be Mothers Day!!!</u> From beginning to end, it had taken just four months!

The funeral arrangements, the ceremony and all, are a blur to me. I wanted nothing to do with it, didn't want to see anybody, and just stayed out of the way. Fortunately, my father and aunt Clara handled the details. Plus, aunt Clara's friend Lena Creanza, who came from the same hometown in Italy (Altamura), took over the cooking chores during this period, and she was invaluable. We had not been friends before, but have been since then, even though we don't live near each other. We still exchange Christmas cards every year, and I'm writing this in September of 2010.

Even in the saddest of circumstances, sometimes there is humor. I was sitting in the parlor with my grief, when my father and aunt Clara returned from making the arrangements at the funeral parlor. I heard aunt Clara telling my father that he had made a mistake. She seemed very agitated, so I went out to find out what had happened. If it was truly a mistake, maybe we could still fix it. Aunt Clara insisted that my father had chosen the wrong casket. He replied that it was a metal casket, and guaranteed to last underground for a long time. She insisted that while that was true, for an extra $50, he could have gotten a casket that had an innerspring mattress! It took a while for this preposterous statement to sink into my head. When it did, together with the oh-so-serious look on her face, it just broke me up. I couldn't get out of house fast enough, and I couldn't stop laughing. I went around the block a couple of times, until I was able to compose myself enough to go back in.

Only two things are memorable to me about the funeral. One was during the funeral procession, after Mass. On the way to the cemetery, it's customary to pass by the house one last time. I was looking out the window of the limousine, at the people and the goings-on. Everything was going on as if nothing had happened! Didn't these people know what a wonderful person we had just lost? My memory snapped back to Corato, and when my brother had died. He had been taken from the house, and the procession had gone through the main streets. We had followed on foot behind a horse-drawn hearse, and the townspeople had all stood aside and bowed their heads to share in our loss. Even the stores shuttered their doors as we passed, to symbolize stopping business. I wanted the same thing for my mother.

The other was at the burial site. She was buried in a plot owned by uncle Larry. The plot was designed to stack four people, and my father's brother Ralph, and aunt Clara's brother Phil were already there. Although the tombstone had only my mother's name on it, I thought it obscene that she should have to share her final resting place with strangers. I wasn't in a financial position to do anything about it, but it preyed on my mind. It stayed there for many years, until Mike and I arranged to have her disinterred, and join my father in an above-ground mausoleum. It gave me satisfaction that I was finally able to do something for the woman who had given so much to me. Even so, I knew it was a case of too little, too late!

## My most shameful decision

Everything had happened so quickly that I didn't have time to analyze anything as it was happening. After the funeral, I was forced to assess the situation that I was in. The first thing that jumped out at me was the fact that running parallel with my mother's physical deterioration, had been Aida's downward moral spiral. She had never been in such a prolonged "depressing" situation, or its accompanying responsibilities. Oh sure, the family had been poor, and had had hard times, but she had been provided for. All she had learned from that experience was to be a penny pincher. We had just had some hard times in Italy, but it had been just the two of us, and I had provided. Plus, her family had come to help during the hard times of her pregnancy, and after Marco's birth. This had been totally different.

During this period, my father had regularly gone to work, Mike and I had regularly gone to school, and aunt Clara came upstairs rarely. So, as my mother regressed, the household chores fell to Aida. She had never had such a responsibility, and was not prepared for it. Actually, it was a full time job for her just to learn to take care of Marco, since she no longer had the help of her parents. So, as the demands increased, she had done less and less, eventually staying in the bedroom practically all day, taking care of Marco. After my mother had become bedridden, I would come home to find that the glass of water by my mother's bedside had not been refilled, the bed not refreshed, and my mother had not eaten anything. My mother was not one to ask for help, and Aida would not voluntarily go to check on her. I spoke to her about it, but it was something beyond her control. She said she just didn't have enough time to do anything other than take care of Marco, and help out with the cooking. Plus, she was doing the wash, and hanging the clothes out on the line to dry.

After my mother was hospitalized, it didn't seem as bad, and we got by. However, it was taking its toll on Aida, and after the funeral, its effect was becoming clearer every day. She had a constant harried expression, and often had that deer-in-the-headlights look. It wasn't good. It was clear to me that she was going to have a breakdown if I didn't do something. I decided that my primary responsibility lay with my immediate family. So, two weeks after my mother had been buried, I told my father and brother that we were leaving, moving to Long Island to live with my in-laws. My father had nothing to say, and my brother was too busy with the loss to care, but I knew. I knew it was a lousy thing to do. I was an adult, and I should have taken over. All the good reasons in the world didn't change that fact. Instead, I saved myself, and left my father and brother to fend for themselves. There hasn't been a year since then that

I haven't reviewed that decision. The answer has always been the same. I would do the same thing today, but it was a lousy thing to do then, and it would be a lousy thing to do now. Again, I had failed my family. It was my most shameful decision.

That decision was important in my life, also because it was the first major break in the relationship between Aida and me. I understood how she felt, I sympathized with her, but I couldn't forgive her. For years thereafter, whenever we would have a disagreement, I would throw that period in her face. With the benefit of the passing years, I can now face the fact that I also could have done much more!

## Life marches on

We moved to Long Island, and lived in the finished basement of the Dammacco house. In case I haven't recorded it before, the addresses were:

739 E. 243rd Street, Bronx N.Y., and 1142 Ferngate Dr., Franklin Square N.Y..

Back with her family, and without the pressures, Aida reverted to her former self almost immediately. I continued to attend NYU days, and work weekend nights at uncle Larry's bar on Simpson Street in the Bronx. We had bought a FIAT 1100 auto, because we had been so happy with our FIAT 600 in Italy. Also, I stayed in frequent touch with my father and brother, and we visited regularly. My father would occasionally take a series of trains and buses to come visit us. He had spent a lifetime going to work as a bricklayer without a car. He didn't speak English well, but he knew the transit system.

Unfortunately, having lost the rudder of the family, my brother also lost his direction. With my father not wanting to pay for the college costs, and my mother not being there to force him to continue, Mike dropped out of school. My father liked the idea because he figured that Mike could then come be a bricklayer like himself, and they could go to work together. As I've said many times, my father was a hard workingman, a devoted family man, but didn't have a whole lot of imagination, and his only goal was to be financially independent. Everything was seen in terms of cost, and our lives would have been totally different but for our mother.

As a matter of fact, my brother did go to work with my father, and did learn to lay bricks, as well as some of the tricks of the trade. The best one Mike learned before he laid a single brick! My father took him up to the wall, and showed Mike "come si frega il compagno", translated as, "how you screw your buddy". This consisted of starting to lay the first row of bricks from the center of the wall, and work towards the corner, instead of the other way around, which was the traditional way. That way, you worked until you met the guy coming from the other end, and then go on to the next layer. In my father's way, you only did your half, and forced the other guy to do his half. The importance of this was that when the foreman came by to look at the job, he could tell who was fast, and who was slow. Since my father was fast, he always looked good. Plus, getting ahead had another bonus. As you went up to the next layer, you lay one less brick, because bricks are laid unevenly. This meant that your "buddy" had to work harder to catch up. The whole thing was compounded, if your "buddy" wasn't experienced, in which case you could cheat on that first row, and start not at the center, but more on your half. If caught, you could always apologize, and say that you had misjudged the distance.

Besides being good for laughs, this system had some very serious and tangible results. It would force the other guys to work harder to keep up, and would result in the walls being finished sooner. This would also mean that the builder would save labor costs for the building. The foremen appreciated people like my father, and he was always in demand on jobs. It was not unusual for a foreman to pick up my father from the house, and drive him to work. He was always one of the first to be hired for a building, and one of the last to be let go. He was most times paid when there was bad weather, and the other bricklayers were sent home. Always, there was extra cash with his regular pay in the envelope. As he said, he owed his allegiance to the bosses, because they put the food on his table. Besides, those guys weren't good bricklayers, and they deserved to get screwed.

Mike didn't last long there. After learning the trade, he had higher ambitions, and decided to go into business for himself. He started contracting jobs for brickwork and home repairs, and hired our father for some of them. He had visions of getting bigger and bigger jobs, but it didn't work out as he had planned. Fortunately, it turned out to be a good thing. There are a couple of funny stories about this period in my "Mikey Stories".

## Mario gets married

Meanwhile, out on Long Island, Mario had taken advantage of his Army training, and gotten a job as a draftsman in a job shop. There, he fell in love with a very pretty and intelligent girl, Nancy Haynes. That was not unusual for Mario, but this time it turned out to be the real thing. It took a while for Nancy to get over Mario's lady-killer reputation, and to trust him, but she eventually came around. When things became very serious, to the point of proposing marriage, Mario became very concerned, and was convinced he was going to lose Nancy. The reason being that, over the years, his hair had started thinning; so much so, that it required "strategic" combing, and not to go out on windy days. Mario didn't want Nancy to marry him under false pretenses, and was sure that she would leave him when she found out that he was balding. He agonized over this for weeks, until he was able to build up enough courage to face her with the truth.

After confessing, he held his breath, and his heart was pounding. It seemed forever before she answered. Surprisingly, she started laughing! She asked him, "Do you really think it's not noticeable that you're losing your hair?" She had known about it from day one, and she had fallen in love with the person that he was. She said more, and you would imagine that this would have reassured Mario, and that he would have started to jump for joy. You would be wrong! That's not our Mario! His reaction was that Nancy was saying this only because she didn't know the extent of his hair loss, and he needed to show her! Days passed, until he built up his courage again. He then proceeded to comb his hair back, and lay his soul bare before her.

Truth to tell, Nancy later admitted that she had been taken aback by the dramatic change in appearance, but it was only momentary. She reaffirmed her love for him, and Mario was finally convinced. They were married on January 24th, 1959, three days later than our anniversary, and it was also Aida's birthday. Aida and I were ushers at the wedding. Over the years, Mario had gotten a new best friend at the job shop, and he was the Best Man.

Mario didn't know what the future held for him, and didn't want any complications (children), until he found out. He wanted to be in control of his life, and made sure everyone knew about it. He made a very big deal of this, before, during, and after the wedding ceremony. He left for his honeymoon well stocked against any "accidents". Donna was born nine months later, almost to the day!

Our in-laws were leaving for Italy, and the house was left for us to use, sharing the expenses. Mario and Nancy had the main floor, and we stayed in the basement, paying $90 a month towards those expenses.

That's the way we ended 1959 and the decade. It's been the most life-altering and intensive decade of my life, and I'm sure I could have written much more about it. Given the time, I'm just as sure that I'll go back and do that sometime in the future. For now, I'm satisfied, and I need to move on. There's much still to happen, and a long way to go.

A thought comes to me as I write this. It seems that my life, at least so far, seems to be running in ten-year cycles, changing course with every cycle. Consider: I was born in 1930; Came to America in 1940; Left home in 1950, with all the adventures just concluded, and 1960 turned out to be another fork in the road. How about that!

*     *     *

# 1960 – 1977

---

*If the 50's were the most intensive years of my life, then the 60's were certainly the most productive, both from a personal and financial standpoint. Mike and I became one, to the point that it seemed like we lived in our own world. In truth, we knew that we were superior, and did live in our own world! That's not to say it was a straight line up, without a lot of curves in the road. The roller-coaster life continued, with many lessons to be learned by us. It could also serve as a tutorial for the reader.*

## Leaving my job at the bar

Jimmy, Vito, and Bernice

The time came when managing uncle Larry's bar became too much for me. The work was fine, but the atmosphere was potentially dangerous. Something could happen from moment to moment.

For example, one early evening, before the usual crowd arrived, I was relaxing in one of the booths, reading the newspaper. Suddenly, a loud argument breaks out at the bar. A guy is yelling at his woman companion. He gets off his stool, takes the beer bottle in front of him, and holding it by the neck, smashes the other end off by a wild swing at the edge of the bar. He then raises the jagged bottle, with the clear intention of doing harm to the woman. This had taken only seconds! I was only a couple of feet away, and in those few seconds, I was able to get out of the booth, get a hold of his right wrist, pull him back and pin him to the wall, and get a firm grip on his other wrist! It was only then that I realized what I had done! I was holding a big black guy, who was as big as me, and holding a broken bottle, pinned to the wall! I was looking into two yellow, watery eyes, and a very pissed-off face! That face was made even more dangerous by the scar that ran from the bottom of his left ear to the left corner of his mouth! Now what do I do?

Fortunately, maybe because he had been drinking, he wasn't able to break my grip. That made him angrier, and he started yelling at me to let him go, with a whole lot of curse words, some of which I hadn't heard before. Well, that wasn't going to happen, if I could help it! As steady as

I could, I looked into those eyes, and told him I couldn't do anything until he first dropped the broken bottle. I had no idea as to what I was going to do if he didn't. We locked eyes for what seemed like an eternity, and then I heard the bottle hit the floor. What a relief! He had actually heard me! Encouraged, I proceeded to explain to him that I couldn't afford to have any kind of trouble in the bar, because I could lose my liquor license and the business. I explained that I wasn't saying he was wrong, but that if he had any problems with his girlfriend, he would have to resolve them outside the bar. I kept repeating variations of this, until the look in his eyes changed, and he stopped struggling. Still defiant, he said, "OK, OK, let me go! NOW!" Well, there was nothing else to do, so I slowly released my grip, and backed up a step at a time, hoping to be giving the impression that I was ready for him. I wasn't. Actually, I couldn't take my eyes off that scar, and wondered how he had gotten it. Slowly, he returned to the bar, took his girlfriend by the arm, and they both walked out. There, they started arguing again. The whole thing didn't last more than a couple of minutes. It's taken me longer to write about it. The old bartender didn't even have time to come out from behind the bar, not that he would have been of much help.

I was sitting back in the booth, breathing a sigh of relief, and trying to not show the shakes, when we heard a commotion from outside. It turned out that the couple had escalated their argument, and the guy had thrown the woman through the plate-glass window of the store next door. The falling glass had done some serious damage, and an ambulance was taking her to the hospital. A police car was taking the guy away in the other direction. Whew!!!

\* \* \*

Another time, it was on a very busy Saturday night. They were standing at least two-deep at the bar, which wasn't unusual. Weekends were for blowing most of the week's earnings, and having a good time. The juke box was playing loud; there was lots of laughing, some serious conversations, and guys and girls trying to line up some action for later on. I would see some guys, charming and well dressed, buying drinks on Friday night, for some also charming and well-dressed ladies. I would see the same group on Sunday night, less charming and more sloppily dressed, trying to mooch back drinks from anyone who had any cash left. Such is the life of alcoholics. I liked these people, and all the stories that I learned about them. There was the black train conductor, who concentrated on enjoying life. Death was not his concern. Somebody would take care of his body. "Do you see any dead bodies lying around the streets? Somebody must be taking them away!" There was the pretty Puerto Rican sister of the barmaid, all dressed-up on Friday, all disheveled on Sunday. There was the Irish guy called "Legs", because he always had a beer chaser with his whiskey. He was a great storyteller, and would talk my ear off. However, if we crossed paths outside the bar, and he was with his wife, he didn't know me at all! There was the well-to-do Jewish hat-maker who philosophized on the corner stool on the weekends he wasn't visiting the kids on Long Island. I was fascinated with them, and thought I would write a book compiling their stories, and call it "From the other side of the bottle".

Anyway, on the busy nights, I would help out working behind the bar. It wasn't hard to be a bartender. Everything was straight. Rye and ginger ale would be considered a mixed drink. One night, from the back of the crowd, I saw a guy waving at me, and calling my name. "Vic, Vic (that was my name), I gotta talk to you! It's very important!" He was waving for me to come out from behind the bar. I didn't recognize him, but he wasn't drunk, and he seemed so very concerned about something. So, I went out from behind the bar, and joined him in the hallway beyond the bathroom door. It was less noisy, with some privacy. I asked what I could do for him. He was Puerto Rican, about a foot shorter than me, and very agitated. He started to tell me a story about how he and a couple of friends were just walking along, minding their own business, when a bunch of white guys jumped them, and beat them up. Beat one of them up so bad, that he had been taken to the hospital. He said he was very, very angry, and wanted to get even. I felt sorry for the guy, but I was puzzled. Why was he telling me this? What did he think I could do for him? I had been looking at his face, listening to his story, but now I happened to look down. I saw him holding the point of a long jackknife to my belly, pushing my shirt button back and forth! I had my arm around his shoulder, but that knife was long and sharp! I realized that if he had intended to do me harm, he would have done it already! So, I sympathized with him, and asked again how I could help him. He said he wanted to get even, and wanted to "stick" a white guy. Since I was handy, it was clear that he was nominating me. Once again, I figured that if he had wanted to do it, he would have done it already. Besides, any sudden move, and that blade could be in my belly in a split second. So, I kept talking, reminding him that I'm not one of those guys, everybody likes me, I'm just like him, a working stiff with a family, that I really felt sorry for him, and that I'm the wrong guy to take it out on. When he seemed to relax a bit, I mentioned that he was apparently a good guy with a family that depended on him, and if he did anything stupid, he'd wind up in jail, and they'd lose him.

I don't know which of those things hit home, or if it was a combination, or if he just lost the nerve. All I know is that the knife started to drop down, and the guy was mumbling, "I know, I know", over and over. So, I started pushing him into the bar area, to get him out of there.

Unfortunately, my "guardian angel" was sitting at the corner stool. I no longer remember his name, but he was a big black guy who wasn't all there mentally. The story was that it was due to the steel plate that he had in his head. So, he always wore a full coat, the inside of which was lined with all kinds of knives, and even a meat cleaver! Everyone knew him, liked him, made allowances for him, and made sure not to disagree with him. He was almost always agreeable, and he liked me very much. He would station himself at the corner stool and say that he would "look out" for me. On this night, he saw the look on my face as we made our way back, and immediately knew something was seriously wrong! He jumped off the stool, faced us both, and in an alarmed voice kept asking, "Vic, what's wrong? What's wrong, Vic?" He started to open his coat! Fortunately, my friend had put his jackknife away, and was too demoralized to pay any attention. I had a quick vision of my other friend going nuts, and doing a saber dance with his collection in a crowded bar. I hugged him with both arms, and assured him that everything was all right. After I got him settled, I escorted the other guy out, and wished him a good night.

\* \* \*

One last story. As I said, everyone liked me, and treated me kindly; especially Bernice, the Puerto Rican barmaid. She even tried to fix me up with her very pretty sister. When I thanked her, and said I was happily married, she liked me even more! So, if a disturbance happened, she made sure I stayed behind the bar. Then she would pass a small bat out to a couple of friends on the other side of the bar, and they would drive some sense into the disturbee. After which, they would throw him out! Her best best friend was her boyfriend "Ace". He was a big black guy, at least a head taller than me, and brawny! He was very easygoing, and would occasionally hang out near the end of Bernice's shift, waiting to take her home.

One night wasn't so busy, and I wasn't behind the bar. While making conversation with "Ace", an obviously drunk person walked in and ordered a drink. I very gently told him that we wouldn't be able to serve him, and escorted him out the door. After a couple of minutes, the guy comes in again, steps up to the bar, and again orders a drink. Once more, I tell him that we can't serve him, escort him out, and walk him down the street a bit. I was surprised and a little angry when he returned once again. This time, I just turned him around, and pushed him out the door. When he turned, and tried to get back in, I locked the door! I didn't know what else to do, but I was also locking out potential customers! While the guy is scratching at the door-window trying to get in, I hear "Ace", from behind me, say "Vic, open the door". I figure he must have a better idea than I do, so I open the door. The guy on the outside, being deprived of a door to lean on, sways a bit. In that instant, a big fist shoots out over my right shoulder, smashing directly into the guy's nose. The fist took up all the space between the eyes and the mouth, and it contorted his features into something totally different from what they had been a millisecond before. I can say this because I had the best seat in the house, and was no more than 18 inches away. It was like watching it in slow motion. What an experience! Well, 18 inches was only momentarily! The gentleman actually flew backwards about fifteen feet, landed on his back, and never moved a muscle. The sidewalk was about 20 feet wide, and he was past the middle. We closed the door, and resumed our conversation. We looked out about ten minutes later.

He still hadn't moved, and people were walking around him. Sometime later, the cop on the beat stopped in to ask if we knew anything about the guy lying outside. We said we didn't have a clue, so he called for a wagon to take him away. When they did, he still hadn't moved!

\* \* \*

There were more incidents, but you get the idea. I don't know how uncle Larry was able to live in this type of atmosphere for so many years, both in Harlem and at the bar. I could say that he had no choice, but that wouldn't be accurate. Others, such as aunt Clara's brother Phil, had moved to less dangerous surroundings. Uncle Larry was there by choice, because it was more profitable. I once asked him why he didn't buy a bar closer to home, like Barneys. He said that it would take a month at Barneys to earn what he did on Simpson Street on one weekend. That's why he was able to pay me so much money.

Be that as it may, I began not looking forward to those weekends. When that anticipation began affecting my schoolwork, I knew it was time to go. I talked it over with uncle Larry, and thanked him for all he had done for me. What I had actually done was to trade one anxiety for another, because now I had no job and no income, but I still had a wife and child.

## My first adult full-time job at Amperex

Let me tell all readers what a boon it is to have family help during hard times. I say this especially to those people who can't wait for their kids to turn eighteen and fly the coop. If these people had been my family, God knows what would have happened to me. My gratitude forever goes to my family, the Mastromauro family when Aida and I went to Italy, and by extension the DeToma family. Back here, we were living in the basement of the Dammaco house in Franklin Square, but it was comfortable, and the Dammacco's were very helpful. At the very least, I knew I didn't have to worry about a roof over our heads. That's a tremendous relief for someone with a family and no job.

All of this didn't lessen my anxiety to get a job. My memory is that this happened near the middle of '59, and it was not a good time to look for a job. I went to many interviews, and saw some engineers take jobs as draftsmen. Since I was attending NYU, I applied for a Junior Engineer position at an electronics firm in Hicksville, which is about 25 minutes away from Franklin Square. Amperex Electronics Corp. was a division of Phillips of Eindhoven, a Dutch company that is best known for its Norelco Electric Shaver. At the time, Amperex was one of 47 divisions scattered all over the place. It specialized in the manufacture of transmitting tubes used in radios and the like. I later learned that they were choosing three people out of 250 applications! The pay was also not very good, starting at $65/wk. Over the next two weeks, I made it to the finals, and the chosen three. Apparently, the quality of the finalists embarrassed the company, and they raised the starting wage to $75/wk.

I was awarded the plum of the three positions, that of assistant to the head Production Engineer, Pat Murphy. The other two were assigned as assistant production foremen, a much more restrictive job, and a step below mine. I had the run of the plant, checking on all areas of production, from beginning to end. Initially, I would just follow up on all the tests and controls that Pat Murphy initiated, and report back on the results. As I became more knowledgeable, I was allowed to make some input in the discussions. Eventually, I was asked to sit in and participate in the weekly engineering meetings. I was assigned some semi-independent chores, which allowed me to become specialized in some areas, such as the bonding of ceramic to metal. It was pretty heady stuff for me. Imagine sitting in a meeting, and having engineers asking my opinion on certain techniques!

There's one that stands out the most, and is also funny. At one meeting, there was concern about the high failure rate of the glass bases being produced, and I was asked to look into it. These bases were made by placing pins in a carbon mold, surrounding them with glass crystals, and then run them on a conveyor belt through a nitrogen-fired oven. The timing included a cooling down period for the molds, after which the bases were removed with bare hands. Unfortunately, about 30%-40% of the production was unusable, because cracks had developed in the glass around the pins.

I compared the procedure with the manual, and found no discrepancies. So, I started looking for variables in the production line, and thought that I had found one. The amount of glass particles being poured in the mold was being measured by volume. That is, they were poured up to a line in a beaker, and then into the mold. To me, this could result in two variables, both of which could affect the amount of glass in the mold. The operator could pour above or below the line in the beaker. Also, there was variation in the size of the glass crystals, so that even pouring consistently to the line could result in more or less glass per mold.

Thinking that I had identified the problem, I proceeded to correct it. I had to change the measuring of the crystals from volume to weight. So, I got a weight balance from another department. On one side I placed the weight of the amount of glass desired. On the other side was an empty beaker. Above was a container of glass crystals, attached to a soft rubber tube that would feed the crystals into the empty beaker. An attachment made it possible to pinch the tube when the exact weight was reached. A heavier weight was then placed on the side of the beaker, so that it could be removed to pour the glass into the mold. Then the procedure would be repeated.

Wahla! I had been right! The failure rate dropped to under 5%, and I was properly complimented at the meeting. I suggested that a more presentable solution should replace my "Rube Goldberg" set-up, and it was agreed to pass it on to the machine shop for execution. Somehow, it didn't get done. As you will read, I later left Amperex to spend a year in Italy. When I came back, my set-up was still there, and I asked why. I was told it was working so well that they didn't want to mess with it.

Working at Amperex was great! I loved the work! Every day was something different, and I was doing engineering work without a degree. Unfortunately, it was also very hard on me! I had switched my classes at NYU to night school. These were all in the Manhattan Washington Square campus, near Greenwich Village. It was a long drive from Hicksville, and a hassle with the traffic. It was so tight that I was always late for a 6:00 PM class. For later classes, I had barely enough time for a donut and a cup of coffee at the Chock-full-of-Nuts after parking. I never got home before 10-11 PM, and I rarely got to see Marco awake outside of weekends, which were spent mostly catching up with my homework.

The problem was compounded by my continued inability to come to terms with chemistry. I just could not get it. I had had problems with it since my freshman year, and no matter what I tried, it didn't work. Augie LaRuffa, a neighbor from Franklin Square, was very bright, and also attending NYU

Engineering. We had commuted together for a while, and he had tutored me with no success. Now it was becoming more serious, and there was no way I could get a degree without passing chemistry.

Furthermore, I realized that I still had a very long road in front of me. Going to school part-time, I wouldn't be getting my degree for at least another four years. I was already 30 years old, with wife and child, and not earning very much money, even though I had been getting raises, and getting close to $100/wk. Now I also had to consider the possibility that I would not get a degree. Clearly, I had to explore alternatives! So, when I got the chance, I sat with uncle Larry to get his advice. His suggestion was to get a part-time route to supplement my income. A route would give me the best return for the money invested. The problem was that I had no money, and when I approached my father about the possibility of a loan, I found that door closed and locked. He still hadn't gotten over the loss of money in Italy. Uncle Larry suggested that I look anyway, to see if anything suitable was out there, and how much it would cost. I thought it would be a good idea to bring Mike in also. He was doing bricklaying work on his own, sometimes using my father, but not making much money, and not having much fun. Besides, he was now 22, and it would feel great to do something together. Mike also liked the idea, and we started to give it some serious thought.

## Starting a business - My father remarries

About June of 1960, my father announced the fact that he was going to Italy, possibly to look for a wife. I was really taken by surprise, but on reflection felt it was a good thing to do. My mother had been gone for over two years, and my father certainly could use some company for his old age. After I came to terms with that fact, I then extended it to consider that it would be a great opportunity for Aida to visit her parents in Italy. She had been living in the basement, taking care of Marco, doing housework, shopping, etc., while I was away doing my "thing" every day, and studying on weekends. Even with the companionship of Mario and Nancy upstairs, it was a lonely life. I felt that she had earned a vacation, but I didn't have any ready cash. So, I went to the bank, and borrowed the money for the trip. All I asked was that she bring me back a Rolex watch to replace the one that I had lost. I had been fascinated by the one that Franco had worn in Italy in 1950. He would wear it all the time, even when spearfishing. I had bought one like it before returning home, and had likewise never taken it off my wrist; through the service, marriage, back to Italy, and through the summer of '59. Then, at Glen Island beach, while playing with Marco, water had gotten into the watch because I had not tightened the winding head. It was not repairable, and it was a big loss for me.

So it was that Aida and Marco sailed to Italy with my father. This made it possible for me to use whatever time I had to spare to check out business opportunities, together with Mike. A route business was not our first choice. The image just didn't have any "pizzaz". A Laundromat or Dry Cleaner did, and we visited a couple that were for sale on Long Island. Unfortunately, they required too much cash down. Uncle Larry's advice that a route would give us the highest return for a small investment forced us to reconsider that area. A friend of Mike's had told him about newspaper morning delivery routes, and he got the name of a business broker on Long Island.

The broker specialized in routes, and suggested we check out a newspaper delivery route in Wantagh. We did, and accompanied the man, Ted Frank, on a delivery run. We met him at three on a very rainy morning. We fitted in his car with him and his newspapers, and took off. We got a history lesson of every subscriber that he delivered to, together with the exact location of where to leave each newspaper. Especially those that got two papers, like the Times and the News! To make sure that we got the feel of it, he told us to make some of the deliveries. For this, I volunteered Mike's services! It was a sight to see him get out in the pouring rain (we had not come dressed properly for the weather), bring the paper up to the porch, look back to get approval that he had left it in the right place, and then get back in the car, looking like a drowned rat! This was repeated many times, because the owner wanted to make sure we understood what was involved. He was precise about everything. He even stopped to point out the tree where he would take a break and pee on every day. There was a whole lot of information, plus all the different newspapers; The News, the New York Times, the Mirror, the Wall Street Journal, even a German and Jewish language newspaper. It was all very confusing, and not in any way glamorous. After leaving, and giving it some very deep thought, Mike and I agreed that it was a great business to get into. Go figure! For years afterward, we were never able to come up with a good reason as to why we had done that, while at the same time being thankful that we had.

The next step was to sit down with uncle Larry. He said that he would be interested in getting into the business, and would advance us the $2000 necessary to get started. Mike remembers that we also had a little money of our own; he sold his Cadillac for $1400, and I could borrow from something called Steady Credit. I trust his memory.

Then everything went quickly, and before we knew it, we were running our own business. Mike would drive out from the Bronx each morning, and we would split the deliveries. Sundays was another matter. There were many more deliveries, and the newspapers were much heavier. To handle this, we paid rent to use someone's garage in the area, and hired a few part-time men, who would help put together and deliver the Sunday editions. During the week, we would process payments received, as well as any addition or subtraction of subscribers, and update the route lists for the following Sunday.

It all sounds very methodical, and gives the impression that we had everything under control. Nothing could be further from the truth. Sometimes, the delivery to us was late for any number of reasons, leaving us with less time to complete our end before people left for work. This was critical! Sundays was even more erratic, and it created a different problem. The part-time workers weren't inclined to hang around forever. They had full-time jobs and didn't want to waste their free weekend time for a few bucks. Breaking in new people was tedious, and the supply wasn't guaranteed.

That was on the outside. On the inside, Mike was driving out every day, and although his mind was willing, sometimes his flesh was weak! After all, he was 22 and single! Hanging out with his buddies until late didn't work well with having to leave for work at 2AM. Girls only made things worse, but I have to give Mikey credit. He was always trying and giving it 100%, especially after messing up in some way. That is, I give him credit now, but at the time, he sometimes would drive me crazy, but it wasn't often; reason being that I was also under pressure. Weekdays, I had to go to work at Amperex, and Sundays was always an adventure, due to the unreliability of the part-time men.

One memory that comes to mind is the Sunday that we were short men, and had to rush to make the deliveries. This made me very short-tempered. After loading up the station wagon, in his anxiety to help, Mike shut the car door on my fingers, which really hurt, and started bleeding a lot. We didn't have time to do anything about it, so I wrapped some newspaper tightly around my fingers to stop the bleeding, and drove off for the deliveries, cursing a blue streak all the while. Being very angry with him, I told Mike to sit on the open tailgate in the back. I would interrupt my cursing to call out the addresses and the newspapers to be delivered, and he would run back and forth, never saying a word, but looking very sorry for what he had done to me. This went on for hours. Eventually, I settled down, and saw the humor in the situation. I even began to feel very sorry for him. There's no way I could stay angry with him for long. We've reviewed that day many times over the years, and it's always good for a chuckle.

Another instance was months later, on New Years morning, which fell on a Sunday. Mike had gone partying the night before, and slept through the next morning. This left me to do his deliveries, so I double-loaded my car and took off. Unfortunately, it was a very bad winter day. Besides the cold, there was a driving storm, a mixture of snow, ice, and water. The visibility was also poor, and I drove into a deep pothole, breaking an axle. No cell phones! So, leaving the car, I walked in that storm, back to the garage, and sat wet and freezing, waiting for help. Fortunately, one of the men came back to clean out his car. He agreed to help me out, so we went back to my car, transferred the newspapers into his, and finished the deliveries. I don't know how I got back home, or why I didn't get seriously sick, but everything worked out OK. Once again, Mike was properly sorry, but I've never let him forget that day!

I should stress that the biggest advantage of the newspaper route was that it left the day free for other work, in exchange for loss of sleep. I still worked full time at Amperex, and Mike kept bricklaying. Thanks to his bricklayers' union card, he was able to get jobs on Long Island. He remembers laying a lot of bricks in Stony Brook, after which he would drive back to the Bronx to see his girlfriend.

It was a tough life, but we finally started to see some extra cash.

\*     \*     \*

That summer was also noteworthy for the fact that I went camping! At Amperex, I had a very good relationship with my boss, Pat Murphy. When he learned that Aida was in Italy, and that I was living alone, he invited me to go camping with his family during the vacation period. Mike agreed to cover for me, and I joined the Murphy family on a trip to Raquette Lake in upstate New York. There, we rented canoes, and paddled out to Big Island, where we set up a campsite. Pat had all the equipment, and I shared a tent with him and his son, while his wife Barbara and young daughters were in another.

What an experience! It was so quiet, that the sound of paddling a canoe was magnified. The nights were so dark, and the stars so bright, because there was no illumination from anywhere! The lake was like a mirror, and the trailing wakes of the canoes could be seen for a mile. At night, we lit a bonfire, toasted marshmallows, and told stories. It was a novel, relaxing week for me. I was sorry to leave. I was told later that on their second week, they had had a night visit by a bear. It had gone through the food tent while they slept. It was proof that food should be kept in a separate place when camping. I was sure that I would camp again soon, but it would be many years before I got back to Raquette Lake.

*   *   *

While all this was going on in America, there was also activity going on in Italy. Aida and Marco, reunited with her parents and sisters, were having a grand old time. Marco was a doll, and everyone wanted to hold and play with him. The old crowd came around, and Aida was having a great summer.

My father, however, was there on business! So, he agreed to be hosted by his sister Maria in Corato, because she had a bathroom! Then, the word was put out that there was an American in town, looking for a wife. I don't remember how I got the information, but there followed a procession of eligible "beauties", none of which stimulated my father. Somehow or other, he was told of a lady that was living in the next town of Ruvo that might appeal to him. So it was that he met Vincenza LaFortezza. She was living in the historical center of Ruvo, caring for her old aunt. For my father, it was love at first sight!

It's easy to see what my father saw! She was a good-looking woman, with all her teeth, and dark hair. She spoke Italian very well, and had a ready laugh. I say all this because it's what I saw when I first met her. On top of it all, she was 44 years old, 22 years his junior! Well, as you and I can imagine, my father's eyes got all curly, and no other woman existed for him.

Now, how about from Enza's side? Mind you, I've never prodded her, and she's only volunteered that she saw him as a good man. I can only conjecture. She wasn't poor or desperate, so I don't see it as an escape. However, she had spent her whole life caring for others. At a young age, she had moved in with her older married sister in Milano. She had spent many years there, caring and helping to bring up the growing nephews and niece. All the time, she didn't have her own room. There was a rollout bed that she would use at night. After the children had grown, she had moved down to Ruvo, to care for her elderly aunt. Somehow, I've heard that there had been a love interest, but that he had been killed during the war. I have no clue as to whether it might be true or false, and I've never asked her. So, I've concluded that she saw my father as an opportunity to finally have a life of her own, with the adventure of coming to America. Plus, my father was still in good shape, and compared very well with men many years his junior. I can testify that in all their years together, she always respected and cared for him. To this day, she remembers those years fondly. Twice, my father was a very lucky man in his choice of a wife!

Mike tells me that in the times that she spent with him and Pat over the years after my father died, she did confide one thing. She had believed that there was going to be very little sex activity in her marriage. She found out that she had been very very wrong. She had even gotten pregnant, but had a miscarriage.

Arrangements were made, and my father and Enza married. Aida and Marco, as well as the Dammacco family, attended the wedding. After which was the filing of the necessary papers so as to allow them to return to America together. During the next 21 years, my father had a wonderful companion to share his life with, as well as the joy of spending time with his grown, successful sons. It was a fitting end to a hard workingman's life.

*   *   *

## Aida's surprised, and another turn in the road

After the summer, Aida and Marco returned. She knew nothing of what had been going on in her absence, so was surprised to see me get up and dress at two in the morning, on the first night of her arrival. I had intentionally wanted to surprise her, and was she ever! I told her it was a business that I had started, and assured her that I would tell her all about it when I got back.

I don't remember exactly when it happened, but something had to give. I couldn't do newspapers in the morning, work all day, and go to NYU at night. I caught a few winks while sitting on a toilet bowl at work a couple times a day. I had started my own business after the realization that an Engineering degree might not be in my future, and I now confirmed that by dropping out of NYU. Of course, this also affected my future at Amperex, but that was a problem for another day.

Mike and I handled the problems, and we began to see some cash. So much so, that when the opportunity presented itself, we bought the adjoining Seaford route. Mike took it as his responsibility, and I took the Wantagh area. We also learned something! The fellow that we bought the route from, whose name was Carbone, did not have the use of his legs. He would drag himself into his car, and never get out. Others would volunteer to put the bundles of newspapers in his car, or he would pull them in with a hook attached to a broomstick. All the deliveries were tossed! This was a revelation to us! No running back and forth and it was so much faster! There was no need to take a break and pee! We resolved that all future new subscribers would be tossed deliveries.

My timeline may not be exact, but a number of things happened in 1961, besides getting the Seaford route. Around February, Aida announced that she was pregnant, and mom and dad Dammacco came from Italy. Mom decided to expand the dormer on the house to a full apartment, for us to move up into. It turned out great! There were windows all around, two bedrooms, an open kitchen, dinette, and den area (with carpeting). We felt like we had moved from the basement to the penthouse.

Gregory was born on August 2nd, 1961. What a difference from Marco's birth. Aida's doctor this time, Dr. Schwartz, believed in painless childbirth. Remember that the Italian doctor Pesce had said that no such thing existed, and that it was "Fesserie Americane"! American nonsense! I wished that I had that shithead by the throat!

Not only was the birth painless, it was by appointment! That is to say that when the time got close, the doctor monitored her frequently. Then, he told us to report to the hospital, Hempstead General, the following morning. There were no pains or contractions, so we stopped off for breakfast on the way. Well, OK, I had breakfast, because Aida was told to fast. Hey, I didn't want to wait on an empty stomach! We checked in at the hospital, and they took Aida away. Once settled, they put her out, and then gave her an injection to induce labor. Aida awoke, and didn't believe that she had just given birth naturally, even though she was looking at her son. As for me, it was also great. After hugging and kissing Aida, and spending time with my hairy second son, I went out for a leisurely lunch. What a difference!

You might be interested in how we chose the name. Well, since we hadn't used my father's name for our firstborn, it would have been disrespectful to him to use Aida's father's name for the second boy. So, we searched for a name that we liked, that wouldn't be mangled or sound funny if shortened. It just so happened, that under a certain light, and seen from a certain angle at a certain time of the day, I had a passing resemblance to the actor Gregory Peck. Even shortened, Greg was a nice name, and so was born Gregory Michael Lepore, to follow Marco Ignazio Lepore.

## An update on Mario

While all this was happening to me, what had Mario been doing with his life? Like me, he was having a heck of a hard time. This was complicated by the fact that every once in a while, his mother would summon him to come to Italy to help her out. He would then drop everything and go, then come back and try to pick up where he had left off. In the back of his mind, he consoled himself with the idea that he would someday be part owner of the pastificio. His future assured, he only had to worry about earning a living in the present. That was turning out to be very difficult.

Up to the time that they were married, both Mario and Nancy were working at the same job shop, Avionics. At some point, a couple of their friend co-workers decided to quit, and start a competing company of their own. Guilty by association, Mario and Nancy were fired. So it was that they went on their honeymoon unemployed, and without a job to come back to.

While on their honeymoon, Mario had been fascinated by some scented candles that he saw in a boutique shop, and thought there was an income opportunity. He tracked down the owner, and made a deal. It didn't turn out to be a winner! There was a similar result with another line of product. Somewhere along the line, he saw an ad for the sale of a car wash in Queens. Meeting with the owner, it turned out to be a deal that he could afford, and Mario began earning money once again.

Unfortunately, life had not been waiting for Mario to find himself. Donna was born in October of 1959, and I was honored to be her Godfather. Money was tight for the both of us, but we shared the house and the daily experiences. As strange as it might sound, we had a lot of fun together, and found enjoyment in those days. An example would be how we both bought Kirby vacuum cleaners.

We were talked into having a salesman come to make a presentation to sell us a very expensive Kirby vacuum cleaner, in exchange for a gift. The presentation was very good, and we were impressed by how many different things this Kirby could do besides being a very efficient vacuum cleaner. For example, it could be used to massage your scalp. The salesman put on the attachment, and chose Mario to demonstrate on. It happened so quickly that Mario didn't have a chance to protest! This was during the time when Mario was still "creatively" combing, to hide the loss of his hair. The salesman turned on the switch when the attachment was about a foot away from Mario's scalp! The transformation was instantaneous! All the hairs stood up at once, reaching for the vacuum, leaving an almost-bald head below! Mario was embarrassed, I was surprised, and the salesman was catatonic! He thought that something had gone seriously wrong with the unit, and that he had just scalped a potential customer!

Once things settled down again, we thought that we were done. However, a final demonstration turned everything around. The man asked us if we knew that there were mites in our mattresses, and how dangerous they were. Secretary of State Dulles had died from them! He then proceeded to vacuum a part of the mattress upstairs, and the one downstairs. After each, he would show what had come out! Disgusting! There was no way that I would ever sleep on my mattress again, or Mario on his! So it was that we each bought a vacuum cleaner that we couldn't afford, and really had no use for. Downstairs, we didn't even have carpeting! To seal the stupidity, after we got delivery of our vacuums, I really don't remember ever vacuuming our mattresses. But forever afterwards, our wives never vacuumed. They always "Kirby'd"!

As I said before, thank God for mom Dammacco. By providing us with a place to live, she had removed the biggest headache from the heads of her son and son-in-law, who were struggling to find their way in life. I appreciated it then, and I appreciate it now. Thanks, mom.

## Mike grows up, and gets married

Just like Mario and I, Mike was also having his experiences. He was only nineteen when our mother died, and his world was turned upside down. His ambition to become a doctor had been dashed, and he was scrambling to find an alternative goal. I can only imagine the kind of anxieties that he went through, but he was determined to succeed. It was the same kind of mindset that he had shown on the bike ride back to Corato in 1950 (Read 1950-1959 Mike and I bike to Trani).

He had worked as a bricklayer, and also done work on his own, before we both got into the newspaper business. That doesn't mean that he wasn't having any fun. He had a good bunch of guys to hang around with, most of them the same kids that I had coached years before. His closest friend was Tommy Rumpf, who had also been a drummer in his band, "The Jesters". He was very outgoing, and made a good match for Mike.

I've always liked Tom. He had had a tough childhood, but had a good heart, and was always entertaining because he saw life a little differently from others. He always felt that you shouldn't take it too seriously. As an example, when I was coaching them, I had them come early in the morning for track practice. This was to teach them discipline, as well as to train. This was not Tom's time to be awake, but he showed up, and went through the drills. He complained that I wasn't giving him enough time to have his morning cigarette, and he couldn't start the day unless he did. When I ignored his request, and told the group to run the quarter mile track, he did so, while smoking a cigarette! He couldn't understand why I got so upset, since he had beaten everyone. You couldn't stay mad at Tom, and he was also a good sport. He was willing to pay for his misbehaviors. As punishment, he once had to dress as a woman, and push a baby carriage carrying another buddy dressed as a baby. They had to parade back and forth in front of the Church, just when everyone was leaving after attending Sunday Mass. The rest of us watched, and it was a sight that was never forgotten.

Much like our group had done years before, Tom had started a conversation with a girl at the window of her apartment, and gotten a date. Having found a girlfriend for himself, Tom asked Barbara to bring a friend for Mike. That turned out to be a problem. Barbara's girlfriend had heard of Mike, and she was hesitant because Mike had a reputation as a "Ladies man"! Can you imagine that? My little brother, that nice kid, had now grown up to be a lady-killer? Well, that's the way it was!

She was persuaded to give him a chance, and that's how Mike met the love of his life, Patricia Termine. She, like Barbara, lived in the building a block away from us, on the corner of 242nd Street and Barnes Avenue. When things started to get serious between them, he brought her to the house to meet our father. He was very happy to hear that she had Italian parents. However, his joy was short-lived when she told him that her father was Sicilian! He was a little relieved when she hurried to tell him that her mother was Napoletana, and said, "Beh, that's all right then". Mike and Pat have been a nice couple, and a great match from the day they met.

I met the Termine family during the summer of '60, when Aida and my father were in Italy. The "Sicilian" father, Anthony, was a hard worker. Besides a fulltime job at the post office, he also had a second job as a milkman. Not having a lot of free time, he needed a good helper to enforce discipline in the family. He had one in his wife Annette! She did double-duty. On the one hand, she wouldn't miss a chance to tell the world how her kids were the best things since apple pie. On the other hand, she made sure that they stayed on the straight and narrow, or they would be reported. They made a good couple, and the family atmosphere was a happy one. Over the years, we've shared many happy days with the Termine family, which was rounded out by Pat's brother Vincent (Vinnie), and sister Barbara.

It was understandable that, given the circumstances, Mike would have a hard time delivering himself promptly to all that was required in our new business. Plus, it was a long commute every day! He managed as best as he could, our financial situation improved, and Mike and Pat were married on October 7, 1961.

They started married life in a nice apartment in Freeport, about twenty minutes away from the business, and Mike was able to concentrate better on the daily routine. That doesn't mean he had an easy time of it; quite the opposite, and it needs to be recorded. It once again proved Mike's determination, when he wanted to do something.

In the process of courting, marriage, car, apartment expenses, etc., Mike found himself in a financial hole. This was in spite of the fact that Pat was working for the phone company, only a couple of blocks away from their Freeport apartment, and Mike had gotten a Newsday estate route to deliver in the afternoon. However, the income wasn't enough to cover the debt payments. It wasn't getting better, and the newly married couple was living from week to week. As an example, they would drive around on Saturday, trying to raise money by cashing checks so as to be able to pay for the newspaper bill on Monday. Then they would try to cover the bad checks. It was a downward spiral, and Mike asked me for help to get out of it. He agreed to live within a strict budget that I set up, and I then contacted all his creditors, making deals to pay them off. The better the deal, the earlier they would get paid. Some debts were settled for thirty cents on the dollar! My memory is that it took about a year to get out of debt, and Mike and Pat lived on the miserly budget that I had set up! They never complained! I was very proud of them both for their accomplishment. Unlike me, Mike had to work for everything he got.

## Another trip to Italy

In the beginning of 1963, an opportunity presented itself. My mother-in-law wrote that she had purchased a villa with many apartments in Trani, and invited us to come spend some time there. For Mario, it was an opportunity to get directly involved in the business of the Pastificio Riscossa.

The car wash wasn't doing all that well, and its days were numbered. For him, the timing was perfect! For me, it was a bit different. The business was going well, and we had some cash. I loved the idea of going back to Trani for a while, living rent-free. Besides, I had never gotten over the bad taste of my business failure there, and thought that maybe I could find a new opportunity. I discussed it with Mike, and worked out a deal for him to run the business while I was gone, while still giving me an income.

So, we began preparations for the move by building two huge crates outside on the sidewalk, and filling it with furniture and stuff. Mario and I decided it would be a good idea to bring an American car there, since they were more comfortable than those tiny Italian cars. There was the problem of getting the car fixed in case it broke down in Italy, but we resolved that deciding to bring two cars! That way, one could be used for spare parts! We thought we were brilliant! So it was that in March we sailed with two huge crates, and two huge 1959 Cadillacs! It was a fun trip. After docking in Naples, we had the crates shipped to Trani, while we drove there in the two Cadillacs.

The villa was great. It was on Via Bisceglie, almost next to the family villa that we had stayed in years before. The two upstairs apartments were for us and Mario, and the Dammaccos had the ground floor. They rented out the other apartments, and there was also a large garage below ground level. Everything was new, and our apartments were already furnished. We settled in, and had a great time. Marco, Donna, Greg, and Michele were always together, and also made friends with the kids from across the way. Most days we ate all together on the terrace downstairs. We went to the beach, saw some of the old crowd, and generally had a great summer.

Marco and Greg

After the summer, there was much less to do. Mario would go to the Pastificio with his parents, and I had a lot of time on my hands. Looking for something to do, I noticed that legume such as lentils and ceci beans were still being sold loose out of a sack. I thought that boxing them would be a good idea, and also a first. Plus, if it worked out, I could work a deal with the salesmen for the Pastificio, who were already in all the Salumerie. First, I had to test-market it, so I registered the business "Lepore Ent." in Bari. Then, I designed and had ½ kilo boxes made, as well as the large cardboard containers to hold twenty boxes. From a wholesaler, I bought sacks of first-quality lentils, ceci, and navy beans. We set up business in the garage below the apartments, and proceeded to fill and glue shut the boxes of legume, using a small scale to weigh the product. Everybody helped, even my mother-in-law. It was funny to see her come home from a day at the Pastificio, change clothes, and come down to the garage, where she would sit, weigh, fill, and glue boxes of legume.

Now for the distribution. Pasquale Chimienti, Angela's husband-to-be, was free, and volunteered to come around with me. He was using family connections to try to get a job in a bank, and wasn't having much luck. Jobs were very hard to get in Italy. This offered him an opportunity for something different, and he had the outgoing personality of a salesman. So, we loaded my Cadillac with boxes, and started visiting the Salumerie. First locally, and gradually enlarging the test area, from Bari to Foggia. We would be gone all day, or sooner if we sold out what we had.

It was a new idea, and the main objection was that they didn't have shelf space available. Pasquale was very good, and we almost always sold out before coming home. The main reason for the failures was that we insisted on getting paid for what we left, while the custom was for the storeowner to have one delivery in hand. Plus, they didn't know who we were. We couldn't afford to do that. The most memorable moment of this experiment came the November night that we were in Bari making a sale. They had the radio on, and the music was interrupted, to announce that President JFK had been shot! The drive back to Trani was filled with updates. By the time we got home, he had been confirmed dead! The news was as big in Italy as it was in the States. It monopolized the airwaves for weeks.

Revisiting the stores after a week or so showed that the boxed legume weren't jumping off the shelves, and there wasn't much reordering. However, the consensus was that it was a good idea, and that it would just take time for people to change to a new habit. Then we got a big break! In Andria, we got to speak to the owner of three minimarkets, which as the name implies, are small supermarkets. He agreed to place a big order, but with two conditions. First, he wanted a lower price, because he sold at a lower price. Secondly, he wanted to pay in thirty days.

I agreed for a couple of reasons. The order dwarfed all the other small sales that we had been making, and it was a way to get the product seen by the most people in the shortest amount of time. The owner agreed to send his truck to pick up the merchandise from our "warehouse". We didn't have enough stock, and everybody was drafted to work. Even my father-in-law. We put in a lot of hours, but the order was ready when the truck came.

After this, I thought that we had done enough of a sample distribution, and sat back to evaluate the results. There may have been some reorders, but none that I can remember. We visited the minimarkets after a couple of weeks, and found the products prominently displayed. However, we were told that sales were disappointing, even with the lower price. When we returned two weeks later to get paid for the order, we got a hard time from the owner. He claimed that it hadn't sold well, and wanted to return the merchandise. Plus, he wanted a further discount, and wouldn't pay the price that he had agreed and signed for.

Suddenly, I was brought back to my previous business experience with Povia, and the people who wouldn't pay their bills, while being hounded by those that I owed money to. I remembered all those anxious days. I started thinking, "What the Hell am I doing here? This country doesn't have enough money to go around, and everybody is trying to screw everybody else." The thought of America, where people paid their newspaper bills promptly (mostly), made me immediately homesick. Italy is a great place to visit, but America is where you want to work! So, I settled for whatever I could get, and started making plans to come back home.

I got quite a bit of use out of my Cadillac, but Mario's stayed in the garage, except for one trip. Mario, Nancy, Aida, and I drove up to Berchesgarten in Germany. That's where I had vacationed while in the service. We took Marco and

Donna with us, and had a great time driving up and back, as well as all the stops along the way. Shortly thereafter, we left for home. It had been a great year, but it was time to get back to the real life. Mario stayed, but I no longer had a good reason.

## Back to work in America

Once back, I picked up where I had left off. While in Italy, I had written to Pat Murphy, my boss at Amperex, to see if there was a job for me there when I came back. Surprisingly, he answered that there would always be a job for me. So, when I came back, I took him up on his offer, and he came through. Since I had dropped out of school, I was no longer an Engineer. However, I had production experience, and was offered the position of production foreman, leading a department of 25 people, mostly women. These were all people that I had worked with before, so it was great.

Mike had done well, and we continued to grow. I made a good deal, and purchased the newspaper route in New Hyde Park. This was the town next to Franklin Square, where we lived. So, Mike and I readjusted the responsibilities and moved on. Our relationship was fantastic. We trusted each other completely, and enjoyed our times together. Besides socializing as a family, we had other fun times, such as our handball games. For example, on Sunday mornings, after having spent all night delivering newspapers, we would come home, change, and go play handball. We would go to a park near us in Franklin Square to play. Mike would come from Freeport, his buddy Tommy Rumpf would drive out from the Bronx, usually with a friend, and we'd play singles and doubles until almost noon. Later on, my old buddy Richie Schultz also started joining us. He and Jeannie had settled in Levittown, not too far away. So, while we were working hard, we were also finding time to play. Mike apparently still had extra time to play on his own, and as a result, his daughter Maria was born in May of '64. My baby brother had not only grown up, but had become a father!

## The Shindig Lounge – Ecstasy, Agony, and Disaster!

Sometime in 1965, we started getting pressure from the Daily News to generate new business. While this was also our goal, we wanted to do it on our terms, not theirs. We distributed all the newspapers, which required weekly updating of the routes. Since the routes were done mostly by memory, we wanted to control the changes so as to minimize mistakes. So, when the Daily News would run promotions in our area, it was a mixed blessing. On the one hand, we got a lot of new subscribers. On the other, it required a lot of processing and memorizing, and it took longer to service the routes while learning. Furthermore, many subscribers would discontinue after the promotion period, and this contributed to the confusion. Nevertheless, we cooperated, and built up our circulation. So much so, that we thought that it would be a good idea to sell the routes while they had these inflated numbers, and get into a more reputable business.

We were fortunate to find buyers for all areas, and were soon cash-rich and free to pursue a new life. I don't remember what else we investigated, but we were struck by an opportunity to get into the lounge business. No, I don't know what that means, either. It just refers to the fact that it was called "The Shindig Lounge", which was a place that played Rock and Roll live music, and had a bar. It was only open four nights a week, Friday through Monday, and was always jam-packed. There were as many people outside, waiting to get in, as there were inside. When our broker showed us this business, Mike and I were bowled over. What was not to like? It was a fun atmosphere, and a great moneymaker. Besides, we had experience in the business, me with the bar, and Mike with the band. It was a perfect match, and we committed ourselves! Unfortunately, there was another buyer!

When our broker told us that they were going to sell to the other buyer, we were outraged! We stormed into their attorney's office while they were negotiating the sale, and made a big scene. So much so, that their attorney accused us of making some very wild accusations, and threatened to have us arrested, and then sue us. OK, so maybe I was the guy with the big mouth! Whatever, we got them to rethink, and wound up making the deal. However, there was one hiccup in the procedure that's worth mentioning.

Our attorney, Ted Daniels, was a nice Jewish lawyer who had been handling all our business, but wasn't familiar with the bar business. The other attorney, I think his name was Schwartz, did nothing but bar business. As part of the sale, the liquor license needed to be transferred from the previous owners to us. This normally would take about a month, during which no alcoholic beverages could be served. Well, this meant that we would be out of business before we got started. Schwartz said not to worry. To speed up the process, he showed our attorney how to put the payoff cash in with the application forms, and the agent to see at the ABC Board. Ted Daniels had never done anything like that in his life, and could lose his license! Schwartz poo-pooed it, and told him there was nothing to worry about. He had done it lots of times, and with this same guy! Since this advice was coming from another attorney, Ted went along with it, but very reluctantly. Maybe he didn't want to be called a chicken from the other attorney.

We weren't sure that Ted would go through with it, so we accompanied him to the State Office Building. All the way, Ted was so nervous that he couldn't talk straight. It got worse when we were directed to the agent's desk, to find that he didn't have his own office. His desk was one of many, in a large area, with lots of people moving about. Our poor attorney had by now become petrified, and had difficulty moving. Actually, he held the manila folder with the applications (and cash) tighter to his chest, and didn't seem to have any intention of letting it go. Fortunately,

Schwartz had called ahead, and we were expected. The agent, still sitting, reached out for the folder, but Ted didn't move. The agent impatiently wiggled his fingers, as if to say, "c'mon". Reluctantly, Ted handed over the folder, and stopped breathing! Mike and I, standing on either side of him, were also affected by the moment, and also got very tense. We were very conscious of the fact that this was a government building, and we could go to jail!

What followed was poetry in motion! We reviewed the moment for years afterward, and remained amazed at the performance! As the folder traveled from Ted's chest down to the agent's desk, I guess because of the tenseness, I was seeing it in slow motion! So it was that I saw the agent open the folder, flip through the application pages until he saw the envelope, and glance inside to see the contents. Then, his desk drawer magically opened, and I didn't see where it went, but the envelope disappeared from the file. Then the folder closed and hit the desk. It had taken only a moment, but it was a symphony! The agent said that he would take care of it, and we left. Ted started to breathe again, and the color returned to his face. We got the license a few days later.

The people that we bought from were three brothers. The memorable one was George, and he called everybody George. It was usually followed or preceded by the word "F_ _ ken". To tell the truth, it seemed that every fifth word that George uttered was "f_ _k". He used it as a noun, a verb, and adjective, etc., but he was a good guy. They all helped us in the transition, but after a few weeks, we were on our own.

The Shindig Lounge was a two-story wooden building in Hewlett, in the five-towns area of Long Island. It wanted to attract mainly the college crowd, and Hofstra University was nearby. Being next to the Belt Parkway, it also attracted the Brooklyn crowd, which was definitely not college material. Most of the time, they stayed out of each other's way, but exceptions were the rule. To help keep things orderly, we inherited a dozen bouncers, who were strategically placed to head off any potential problems, and settle any that did arise. They were very zealous, and most customers that were carried out were bloodied only because they hadn't behaved when they had been told to do so. The fire department had hung a sign that approved the building for 495 occupants, but if you looked close, you could see that the original number was 295. Whatever it was, the place was packed, it rocked, and the parking lot was filled with people waiting all night to get in. We were told that drugs were helping to pass the time outside, as well as inside the building. After each weekend, bathrooms had to be routinely unclogged, and punched holes in the walls repaired.

We didn't learn about the seedier aspect of the business until we were in it. We were visited by the local police chief early on, and were advised that we were under surveillance. We assured him that we wanted to run a clean place, and would cooperate any way we could, but I don't think he believed us. In fact, we did try. Double proofing, quicker to kick out troublemakers, a closer eye on people in the bar, were some of our first attempts. To tell the truth, it was hard to try new things, because we were too busy trying to control the flow of humanity, and counting the money!

At the beginning, it seemed like we had stepped into a gold mine! There were young people everywhere, very loud music, and orderly confusion. There was an entrance fee of two to three dollars just for the privilege of getting in. The accumulating singles quickly became burdensome, and we would relieve the door-checkers of the money a few times during the course of the evening. We would lock the money in the office safe upstairs. I can't tell you how wonderful it felt to make those trips to the safe, pockets bulging with cash. At the end of the evening, the cash was counted out. Then, a few of the bouncers would go make a night deposit to the bank, which was in the mall across the street. We got used to it very quickly.

Actually, Mike and I had started to divide our responsibilities. Since he was closer to the age group of our patrons, he did all the socializing with them. Plus, because of his musical knowledge, he also handled relations with the bands. I handled the nuts and bolts of the business, and the arrangement worked out very well. We regularly compared notes, and decided together on what to do next. Surprisingly, I was still working at Amperex. Since our business was in the evening, and on weekends, I was able to do both, but it was tiring. However, given the success that we were having, the job became less and less attractive, and I soon gave my resignation. I was very sorry to leave Amperex. I had enjoyed my years there, as well as the people that I had worked with.

As we became more comfortable with the new business, we began exploring ways to make it more successful. The first area to explore was how we could make more use of the building. We were open only a relatively few hours a week, so we tried adding a night. That didn't go well. We tried opening on Sunday afternoon, to watch pro football on TV, serving burgers and fries with the drinks. That wasn't worth the time spent. We tried for the teenage crowd, opening on Saturday afternoon, with a live band, and serving non-alcoholic drinks, but that also seemed a lot of work for the money it brought in. Truth to tell, we were spoiled! On weekends, we stood there and picked up $1000-$1500 just for letting people in. The profit on the bar drinks was also great, and the sum total was easy money. So, we turned to streamlining the operation.

Mike, who was never short of ideas, kept coming up with new ones. One that worked well was the "Band Tryout Night". All bands have their groupies, even the ones that haven't recorded anything. We had a finished second floor that was not being used, so we put the word out that the bands could come to "audition". I was amazed at the number that responded! Mike scheduled their appearances, usually two per night, and evaluated them. He made it clear that their value was not only in how well they played, but how many fans they would bring with them. So, we got new people in, and they had to pay, even though they were there to watch an "audition". This added a sizable number to our crowd, with free music. What made it even better was they were not on the main dance floor downstairs. The bands were happy because they were getting exposure, and we were happy because we were earning extra money. The regular crowd also liked to check out the fresh meat, and our regular band was aware that there was competition in the house. It was a win-win situation for us.

We would regularly project films of surfing competitions, which were very popular. Some of our bouncers had black belts in karate, so we had their school give a demonstration on our dance floor. A fellow that had worked with me at Amperex had also been a theatrical agent, and he arranged for some vocalists to also come out to "audition". We also paid for some performers, as well as for "go-go dancers". I mention these things to show that we weren't just sitting still collecting cash. In fact, we tried to bring more class by adding tables and waitresses, but it just wasn't that type of place. We even scheduled a New Year's Eve special upstairs, and hired a TV personality of the day, Clay Cole, to perform. Mario, Nancy, Mike, Pat, Aida, and I celebrated it together. It was marginally successful.

I wasn't much into the music, and concentrated on the money. Mike still kids me about the time one of the singers from "The Four Seasons" came into our place. He was accompanied by a large group, who kept trying to impress me with who the guy was. I told them I didn't know the guy from Adam, and if they wanted to come in, they all had to pay. The guy never said a word, but from the way he smiled when he paid, I knew I had just made a major goof! I consoled myself by counting how much those guys had just paid. Mike also had a memorable moment. You can read it in "Vito's Journey" under my "Mikey" stories. It's called, "To hold, or not to hold."

**An offer we couldn't refuse**

We were doing well, when we received another offer. Talk about the embarrassment of riches! Mike got a call from a representative of The Daily News circulation department. We had left with a very good reputation, and they wanted to enroll us in a new program that they were going to launch. We agreed to listen, and went to a meeting with the executives at The Daily News building in Manhattan. We learned that The News intended to distribute to its home delivery subscribers independently. It didn't want to be delivered with other newspapers by independent dealers, such as we had been. They were initiating a Franchise system, with exclusive territories. The Franchise dealer would not be an employee. He would retain his independent status, but would not handle any competing newspaper.

There was a franchise contract, and some very attractive incentive programs for the start-up. Plus, the purchase price was ridiculously low, $3000. Since we were one of the first called, we had the choice of area. They showed us the map of Long Island, with all the areas delineated, and gave us some time to make a decision.

We were doing well, but this was too good a deal to turn down. Plus, we weren't working that many hours, and the hours didn't conflict with those required for newspaper delivery. We agreed that it would be a great second business, and started driving around to choose our exclusive delivery area. We felt like the '49 settlers, free to stake a claim anywhere we wanted. The world was our oyster. We wanted a blue-collar community with money, and also checked store sales of The Daily News to determine the prime areas. We settled on the adjoining areas of Bay Shore and Brentwood, and signed two Franchise Dealer contracts with The Daily News. As a condition of that contract, we had to rent an office, the cost of which would be subsidized. We found a centralized location on Brentwood Road in Bay Shore, and we were in business. To be more specific, we had contracted to start a business. We had zero circulation, in an area already being serviced by independent dealers, such as we had been the year before. That would seem like scabby behavior, and I'm sure that's how the independent dealers saw us. However, it wasn't our idea, and if we didn't do it, someone else would!

There was another major wrinkle that divided our methods of operation. While the independent dealers employed adult carriers, using cars and tossed delivery, we had contracted to use only carrier boys. This was a totally new concept! Not the use of carrier boys, but that they would deliver newspapers before going to school in the morning! No one was doing it, and even to me, it seemed like a barbaric thing to do to children so young (12 to 15 years old). Our feelings were confirmed by the local school boards. When word got out of what we were planning to do, the various boards had emergency meetings, and unanimously voted that this was not a good thing for children to be doing. Letters were sent to parents vilifying us. It was not a good way to start!

We weren't bothered too much by all the commotion. This business was just a hobby to earn a few extra dollars, with minimum effort. So, we participated in the promotions, took the money, but weren't really doing very much. We assigned one of our big, burly bouncers to the job. He would go out in the morning, and toss free sample newspapers in a designated area. After two or three weeks of such delivery, we would give the Daily News representative the addresses being sampled. They would then telephone the area, soliciting for subscribers. This was followed up by foot crews canvassing the area for additional customers. All the while, we continued to deliver free samples in the area. As you can see, it was a very time consuming process. It was one that we had proposed, and because of our experience, the rep went along with it. The other dealers didn't enjoy the same freedoms that we did, and we were in no rush! We were subsidized for every newspaper delivered, and paid a bonus for every customer generated. It was like shooting fish in a barrel. It wasn't a lot of money, but it was easy money.

Mickey Kasis, our burly bouncer, was perfect for the job! He didn't ask any questions, was reliable, and did a good job. His size discouraged angry dealers from confronting him. Although, one time, he arrived to find the newspapers tinkered with. Maybe "piddled" would be a better word. He felt compelled to file a police report of the incident. When we arrived later on, we checked with the precinct for an update. We spoke with the officer who had taken the report, and he couldn't stop smiling while he told us of the conversation that he had had with Mickey. He had been impressed by how concerned Mickey sounded, but didn't know how to advise him on what to do. The officer had asked for a description of the damage done to the newspapers. Mickey, in all seriousness, had responded, "Sir, there are a lot of bundles of newspapers here, and they have all been peed on. In all honesty, I must tell you, it looks like it was more than a one-man-job!" This became a classic story to be shared with those in and out of the business.

## Marisa is born

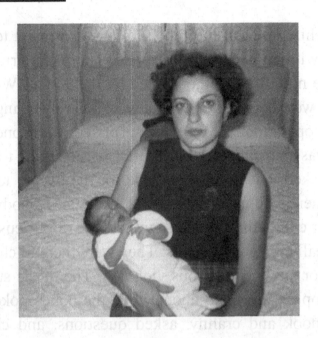

About this time, Marisa was born, on August 22, 1966. As with Gregory, it was a painless birth, by appointment, this time at Franklin General Hospital, which was just a few minutes away from the house. As with Gregory, Aida was totally surprised to be handed a baby, and told that it was all over. Once again, we reviewed the "barbaric" way that Marco was born, and thanked God for American doctors. This time, choosing a name was easy. Both grandmothers were named Maria, so we wanted a variation of it. We narrowed it down to Marina or Marisa. We rejected Marina because it is also a dock for boats.

## <u>My night in jail</u>

Meanwhile, back at the ranch, things continued to move along, with an occasional surprise. The most jarring one was the night that we got raided by the police! We knew that we were being watched, but were honestly trying to run a clean operation. So, we were surprised when, one night, there was an invasion of blue uniforms. As usual, the place was packed, but room was made for the twenty to thirty policemen, who put the place in lockdown! Nobody could leave or come in! We also saw that four of our customers were really undercover cops. They were there to check for drugs, or any other serious violation. The music stopped, and people just milled about while the police poked into every nook and cranny, asked questions, and checked identities. It was very intrusive and uncomfortable for us, and our people, but I didn't see what we could do. Mike on the other hand, got very excited! Maybe because he socialized more with the customers, he felt more personally violated.

When about forty-five minutes had passed, and the police still had found nothing, Mike started to yell at the cops, "You can't do this! You can't do this! I'm copying down your badge numbers! Who's in charge? I demand to know who's in charge?" When an officer stepped out and asked him, "Who's in charge here?" Mike calmed down, and we looked at each other! I asked the officer how much longer this was going to go on, and he replied that we had served liquor to a minor at the bar, and was arresting the bartender and me! The minor had double proof, but it was phony. We were led outside, handcuffed, and placed in the police car. Mike followed, and he looked so sad that I actually felt sorrier for him than for myself. I told him to call our attorney, Ted Daniels, and have him come to the station to get me out.

At the Mineola police station, the bartender and I were processed and fingerprinted. When my attorney didn't show up, I called him. He said that he couldn't do anything till morning. I then asked where he was at the moment. He said he was in bed. I asked him if his wife was in bed with him. He said yes. I asked him if he was nice and warm. He said yes. I then told him that that's the way I wanted to be, in my nice warm bed, laying next to my wife, so get your ass up and get me out of here! He patiently explained that he would have to make up some papers, find a friendly judge, go to his home and wake him up so he could sign the release, and then come to the jail to get me out. It was already the middle of the night, and even if he were successful, it would be morning. On the other hand, I was scheduled to be arraigned first thing in the morning. He guaranteed that he would be there waiting for me, and that I'd be out immediately thereafter. I knew that he was right, and agreed to wait. He then begged me to call my brother, and tell Mike to stop calling him every five minutes!

Mike was still at the lounge, and all he could say was, "I'm sorry! I'm sorry! I'm so sorry!" I knew how badly he felt, but there was nothing for him to be sorry about. That didn't stop me from razzing him for years afterward. Anyway, having accepted the fact that I was going to spend the night in jail, I tried to make the most of it. It was easier said than done. I was assigned a cell to myself, complete with toilet and sink, all open to view. There was also a slab of wood, which served as a bunk. No mattress with sheets and a pillow, just a slab of wood. Plus, they had taken the shoelaces from my shoes, as well as my belt. I had on only the pants and shirt that I had been wearing at the club. This wasn't very warm on a cold winter night, and all the windows in the cellblock were cracked open. As I sat on my wooden bunk, I tried to get warm by increasing my circulation. I vigorously started to rub my face, my arms, and my chest. The cells were being monitored by a video camera mounted on a rod that would slide back and forth, the length of the cellblock. The stillness was broken only by the whirring sound of the moving video camera. I heard it coming, and I heard it going, as it passed my cell. Then, I heard it stop, and come back to my cell for a second look! I quickly realized what I had done wrong! Unfortunately, when it had passed the first time, I was in the process of furiously rubbing my thighs! I could see how they could have misinterpreted those actions. Sure enough, I heard the end door open, and three officers rushed down to see if they indeed had some kind of pervert on their hands. I sheepishly explained what I was doing, and asked them to at least close the windows. They were obviously irked at having had to come and check on me, possibly taking them away from their all-night card game. They left without a word, and the windows stayed open.

Surprisingly, after a couple of hours of this on and off activity, the wood that I was sitting on felt softer! So much so, that I actually lay down, and fell asleep! I must have been in a deep sleep for all of twenty minutes, when I was shocked awake! The duty officer was waking everyone up by walking down the cellblock, running his billy club along the cell-bars. Since those bars were only a couple of inches away from my head, I thought that my brain had just exploded! The officer then announced that we would be leaving for the courthouse in a while, and should start getting ready. Then he passed around stale Danishes and coffee. I thought that was a nice thing for them to do. When the time came, the cellblock doors slid open; we tenants stepped out, and were promptly manacled to each other. Then, we were marched out to a waiting van, and a trip to the courthouse. It was my first chance to see who I had spent the night with. Actually, I smelled my fellow boarders a little before I saw them. Now, being handcuffed together, the stale alcohol was almost overpowering. Now I knew the reason as to why the windows had been left open, and was very thankful.

After a brief ride to the Courthouse, we were escorted into an adjoining waiting room, bounded by a chicken wire.

The cuffs were removed, and my disheveled friends and I waited our turn to go before the judge. When my name was called, an officer escorted me into the courtroom, and up to the judge. On the way, I passed the bench that Mike and Ted were sitting in. They both had a very somber expression on when I was looking at them, but as I passed and shifted my attention forward, I could still see them out of the corner of my eye. I saw them both put their hands to their faces, and their bodies started shaking! They thought this was very funny! Ted stopped laughing long enough to come and stand beside me, and tell the judge what a wonderful person I was. He did the same for our bartender, and we were out of there in no time. Once outside, he confessed that he had sneaked a peek, and that the sight of me in that chicken cage with all those drunks, was the funniest thing that he had seen in his life. I corrected him, reminding him that the funniest thing really was his face, when he was paying off the ABC agent! That shut him up. Mike was harder to do. His face kept alternating between deep sorrow and guilt for what he had put me through, and how funny I had looked in the cage. He said it was all Ted's fault. He didn't want to look, but Ted made him! Now that I was out, I could also see the humor.

## A turn for the worse

If we had known then what we would find out later, we could have saved ourselves a lot of money and grief. Rock and Roll was a fad, the flavor of the day, and depended on change to keep the disciples interested. As noted, we were trying new things, but passed on others. One was electrified plastic blocks, with which you could build a wall or a dance floor. Each block illuminated with a different color and intensity, depending on the different beat and instruments in the band. It made for a great kaleidoscope, but it was too costly for us. However, some other places put it in, because we got reports of it. We lost a few of our steady customers, but weren't overly concerned, because of our long waiting lines outside. Soon, we learned another lesson. Most of those people waiting outside had no intention to come inside. They were having fun out there, and getting "action", without having to pay anything. They could also booze and party without being hassled by the bouncers.

The knockout punch was administered by the well-known disc jockey of the day, Murray the K! Murray was also a promoter, and exploited his fame by getting into our business on a large scale. On Long Island, he rented out an empty hangar in Roosevelt Field, and turned it into a dance palace. With his connections, he could provide class bands. The place could handle a thousand people, so the entry cost was compatible to the competition. The competition? There was no competition! It dwarfed the competition!

We heard of what was going on there from our regulars, who had visited, and reported back to Mike. Gradually, they stopped coming back! We also learned another lesson. These people traveled in packs, and when you lost one, you lost a bunch! It wasn't long before there was room on the dance floor, and few people waiting outside! Another lesson learned; if the place was packed, people wanted in. But, if they peeked in and saw space, they would move on to another place! It became like a monster, the losses feeding on itself, leading to further losses.

We then became aware of something that had not been a concern; our overhead expenses! $1500 a night seemed like a lot of money, especially when it was mostly in singles, and quickly filled the pockets that were emptied multiple times a night into the office safe. However, as the $1500 became $1000, and then $500 and still sinking, the expenses became a nightmare! We had a big rental bill, and big personal notes to the sellers. Because of the type of business, the insurance premiums were very hefty. The pay for all the bouncers, the band, and other help was also significant. Add to that the repair bills and other maintenance, and the payments became much more than what was coming in. For me, it brought back the bad memories of Italy and the Bar Centrale. For Mike, it was his first experience, and he wasn't taking it well. It all registered on his face.

The money started going out much faster than it had come in, and we were drawing from our past earnings. It was decision-time. What to do? We had to change the format, but to what? The first option that we thought of was to become a topless bar. A place in Manhattan had done so a few months earlier, generating a lot of publicity, and we would be the first on Long Island. There would also be a lot of legal challenges, so we met with our trusted attorney Ted Daniels. After research, he said he was ready, and that it would be OK so long as the girls had pasties on their nipples. At the last moment, we decided against it. The bad publicity that it would generate would not be worth it. We weren't those kinds of people, and didn't want to expose our families to it.

The vendor that owned the cigarette machine and the coin-operated pool table was "connected", so we were approached to be a front for a mob-run operation. That was also rejected. Then we were approached to become the first gay bar in the area. We actually met with two of their representatives, and they made a good case. The gay community was large and affluent, and there was a shortage of places where they could congregate. Any place that they endorsed would become an instant success. We were seriously interested, but turned it down for the same reason as before. We weren't those kinds of people, and didn't want to expose our families to the bad publicity.

Mike then got the idea to go a new way. Since all the fads started on the West Coast and came east, he checked in that area. It was the era of the flower children, protest songs, peace, and drugs. So, he suggested we go that way, without the drugs. I thought that it was enough of a change to bring our people back, and worth a try. We shut down for a couple of weeks of renovation. Renovation might not be the right word, since we didn't have much money to spare. However, we put our bartender to work, putting a coat of paint on the outside. Then, Mike commissioned a spaced-out customer to make a few murals in colors that would respond to ultra-violet lighting. Then, a lot of what looked like pieces of eggshells attached to a short string, were hung from a black-painted ceiling. A lighted mirrored revolving ball would add to the fantasy. For the major attraction, he arranged to get a contraption from a guy in Greenwich Village in lower Manhattan. I went down to pick it up, and it was an experience!

I had never been there, and Greenwich Village was an experience! The place was on the second floor of the address given, but I had a hard time getting to the door. Reason being that there was almost no light, and the floor was strewn with people lying on straw mats, recovering from whatever they had ingested, or injected. Once I got in, it was another sight. It was a humongously large room, with large windows, and a very tall ceiling. In the midst of it was scaffolding made of pipes, much like giant monkey bars from the playgrounds. Across the middle of those pipes lay a couple of planks with a mattress on it. There, the disheveled artist lay, contemplating his next masterpiece. He climbed down to meet me, and escorted me to an adjoining room, which was as dark as it was in the hallway. The floor was filled with similar straw mats. In the center was a sealed plastic cylinder filled with fluid, with things floating in it. I was told that it was mineral oil, and the objects were pieces of photographic film. With the push of a button, the cylinder stared rotating. A projector shone a light through the revolving film, creating an ever-changing scene on the screen mounted opposite. Sometimes you saw a face, and then it would change into something else. It was truly mesmerizing! Now I understood the reason for the mats on the floor! I was told that those people outside were regular practitioners, and that they saw the visions almost as a religion! I had stumbled into a church for the stoned!

The artist assured me that he would come out to set up the thing in our place, and I left, but I didn't believe him. Son-of-a-gun showed up a couple of days later, and did as he had promised. We set it up upstairs.

We also met with the owners of Serendipity, in Manhattan, to see if they would serve at our place. It was the "in" place in the city, and would have generated a lot of publicity. However, the owners didn't want to expand. We also made an attempt to set up a boutique shop in the foyer entrance, but it didn't amount to much. Finally, the day of the reopening came! We had been working up to the last minute, and were totally worn out! So-much-so, that we couldn't go downstairs for the opening. It went on without us. We were holed up in our office upstairs, still grimy and dirty from the last-minute repairs. We were eating a sandwich, when we were interrupted by a woman reporter from "The Village Voice", who wanted to interview us about our place, which had been appropriately renamed "The Hip Trip." I was embarrassed to be seen in that condition. Even more so when I realized that my pants had split in the crotch area, and my underwear was showing. However, there was nothing that could be done about it, and we proceeded to answer her questions. We were interrupted by the phone ringing. Aida was calling. She was all excited, and couldn't wait for me to get home to tell me! She had gone shopping that day, and had come across a fantastic deal! She had bought a spoon-holder for a dollar!

It was funny because I had intentionally kept the bad news away from her. I wanted my personal life separated from my business life, but this was ridiculous. I was a victim of my own success!

Curiosity brought people in for a look. It was different. The kaleidoscope upstairs generated a lot of buzz, as did the murals and the dancing lights, and the bartender with the granny glasses. However, few returned, and it turned out to be a brief flicker before the flame went out altogether. It could have been worse, but our poverty saved us. We owned nothing, so our suppliers were stuck. The previous owners had our personal notes, and we met with them. They became convinced that we weren't hiding any money, and that coming after us would be like throwing good money after bad. So, they let us off the hook. However, they stayed in the back of my mind for many years. They had kept the notes, and what was to stop them from trying to collect when we would be flush? All they had to do was check on us every few years. Fortunately, they never did.

The Shindig Lounge was a rocket ride! Went up fast, and came down even faster! The whole thing lasted a little over a year, and I was broke! Again!

## Up from the ashes

The loss of the Shindig Lounge was harder on Mike than it was on me, even though we may not have realized it at the time. Sure, I was broke, and so was he. Sure, I had a family, and so did he. However, I was living in my mother-in-law's house, and if worse came to worse, she wouldn't kick me out. Not so with Mike and Pat, who were living in a nice apartment with a big monthly rent. He didn't have rich in-laws to fall back on. Mike, true to his nature, didn't dwell on the loss. As soon as the Shindig Lounge became history, he diverted his full attention to the new business.

The framework of the new business was in place. We had an office; we had previous experience, and had a plan. There was a lot of promotional money available, and we had been dragging our feet. Now, freed from any other obligation, we started to make up for lost time. We worked nights delivering newspapers; bundles for carrier boys to deliver, and sample copies for new areas. Then home to sleep for a few hours. We were back at the office later in the day for paperwork, and out canvassing the streets for prospective new carrier boys. This was the part that I liked the least, and never got used to it. I still had that feeling that kids shouldn't be delivering newspapers in the middle of the night, and felt like some kind of degenerate in trying to talk them into it. Truth to tell, it wasn't up to them. They had to get their parent's permission. Still, it bothered me. That's why I always felt that our kids were a special breed, and far above those kids who delivered Newsday in the afternoon.

Amazingly, we made giant strides in a short time. So-much-so, that in a year's time, the Shindig Lounge had become nothing more than an unpleasant experience, and a distant memory. Shortly thereafter, we became the largest franchise on Long Island; the first and only one to exceed 2000 in circulation. To appreciate what a big deal this was, you must know that The Daily News was not a local newspaper. That distinction belonged to Newsday, which was also a well-run operation, and almost in every home, or so it seemed. On the other hand, The News was a city newspaper, with maybe a couple of pages of local coverage. With time, the coverage increased, but it could never compare with Newsday. So, in most cases, the subscribers were also getting Newsday. The biggest selling point for The News was that most Long Islanders had moved out from some part of New York City, and felt an attachment to it.

Our growth didn't come without arguments. Not between Mike and I, but with The Daily News representatives. Mike and I got along great, and although we may have differed in discussing methods and approaches, we always agreed on the final decision. The problem was that The News' primary goal was to increase circulation, while ours was to expand in a controlled and profitable manner. In the first couple of years, there were many examples of dealers that had tried to operate the way that The News wanted, but had been unable to handle the business generated. Burnt out, they had lost both their business, and their money. Unperturbed, new dealers were found, and the push would continue. To be fair, it must be mentioned that the reps were salaried, and that their performance was evaluated primarily on how much circulation they put on each week.

So it was that Mike and I developed a strategy that served us well. As we had done at the Shindig Lounge, we divided our responsibilities. Mike would be the primary contact with The News, and my primary concern was to run the day-to-day operation of the business, and implement any new decisions that we had arrived at. Furthermore, we did the good cop-bad cop routine with The News reps. I would get angry, and tell them off. Mike would then go in and make peace, and negotiate the settlement that we had wanted in the first place. In this manner, our operation kept growing to the point that we needed help. We hired our first secretary, Marylyn Becker, for the office work, and to deal with the carriers. She soon needed additional help, and recommended a friend, Marlene Auerbach. At our zenith, we had almost a hundred carriers. Somewhere along the way, the law was changed, and girls were allowed to deliver newspapers. By this time, all new carriers were generated by word-of-mouth, and Marylyn maintained waiting lists. No more canvassing the streets. We had two vans, and hired drivers to deliver the newspaper bundles to the carriers. We had come a long way from our first newspaper route. It was now an honest-to-God business, with an office and everything. We became even more settled when the opportunity presented itself for us to buy the corner property, which was two doors away from our office. The office was as large as the one that we were renting, but it had more usable property, with a large parking area. It was a great deal! My memory tells me that we bought it for $12K.

As I've already said, our relationship with The News tended to be confrontational, but there was no denying our successful methods. From the beginning, we were winning awards such as a Florida vacation and top cash awards. We were even lucky, and won a car in a lottery from among the top performers. We already had new cars, and didn't know what to do with it, so we took the cash alternative.

## The Co-op City expansion

Although we operated in Suffolk County, our reputation was well known at The Daily News Building in Manhattan.

So, when a unique opportunity presented itself, we were solicited. There was a large tract of land in the Bronx, which had once been an amusement park called Freedomland, and was now going to be developed for housing. It was going to be called Co-op City, and would eventually be home to fifteen thousand people. The News was assigning a franchise to it, and wanted us to take it. It was a great opportunity, if for no other reason than that in the Bronx, The News was the primary newspaper. No Newsday! Oh sure, there was the New York Times, but that was a different readership. We accepted, and adjusted our contracts. I became the franchisor for Bay Shore/Brentwood, which freed Mike to sign for the one in the Bronx.

Buildings were going up one at a time, and families were moving in in a controlled manner. We met with the CEO of Co-Op City, and established a working relationship. We got the tenant move-in schedules, and Mike met with the art department of The News. A set of unique flyers was developed for the program. These were given out with free newspapers to the incoming tenants, so that the first thing that they would see when they entered the apartment for the first time would be our newspaper. Just as we had done on Long Island, these free copies went on for weeks, until we had been able to solicit everyone in person or by telephone.

Since Long Island was able to run itself, Mike and I devoted ourselves to physically delivering the samples, with the promotions, to make sure it was done the way we wanted.

This led to a funny story. We received a note from one of the new tenants, thanking us for the free newspapers, but asking us to please stop delivering to them. They were Jewish, and did not read English. The accumulating newspapers were just so much garbage that they could do without. They were elderly, and could do without having to carry the extra weight to the garbage bin, so please stop. This was easier said then done. We weren't programmed for individual service, so although we read the note, we forgot the request. However, we were reminded of it one morning when, as I was sliding the newspaper under an apartment door, I heard a wail from the other side. With a heavy Jewish accent, I heard, "Oyyyyh Mabel, here it comes again!"

Our program was tremendously successful, even more so because the buildings were going up before the stores were occupied, and we had no competition. At a progress meeting with The News executives, they were astounded at our subscriber rate, which was at about 90% of the population. Of course, as things normalized, so did the percentage, but we had done very well. We established an office with a warehouse, and Marlene agreed to commute from Long Island and manage the office operation.

To further take advantage of the situation, we solicited the New York Times for the area, and got it. We got around the contractual violation with The News by having me sign with the Times. My contract with The News was on

Long Island, a totally different geographical area. This contributed to the love/hate relationship that we had with The News. I will give you an example to illustrate it.

The News spent a lot of money trying to generate new subscribers. Most of it was done by telephone solicitation, and orders generated in this fashion were very expensive for them. So, it was understandable that they would want every order generated to be serviced immediately. Moreover, since they were being given to the dealers free, we were expected to do as told, and say thank you. In theory this was great; in fact, not so much! Reason being that the quality of the orders was very poor, with a high percentage of outright phony orders. This resulted in a lot of churning of subscribers, putting them on one week, only to be taken off the next. The carriers were saddled with a lot of extra work, and lost money when they couldn't collect. We reimbursed the kids when they told us, but I'm sure it wasn't reported 100%. On the other hand, The News rep was perfectly happy when we increased our order with the phony business, but gave us a lot of static when we wanted to cut our order the following week. Many dealers were browbeaten into carrying and paying for those papers, but not us! We started verifying every order received, and processing only the good ones. Every week it was a battle royal, with me carrying on and telling the reps where they could shove their phony orders, and I even volunteered to shove it up there for them! At the proper time, enter Mike (the velvet glove), with an offer they couldn't refuse! He met with the bosses in Manhattan, and convinced them to pay us the same premium per order as they did to their contractors, and we would generate our own business. This is what we had wanted to do in the first place. So, we set up some extra phones in our side office, hired some telephone solicitors, and started a new business. Once again, it was a win-win situation. We started earning extra money just for generating new business, which would then generate more income as additional subscribers. The News was happy because there were no more arguments, and the quality of the new business was very high. So-much-so, that we were asked to start soliciting in a couple of other dealer areas, in competition with their contractor. We did much better. We then set up a telephone canvassing room in the office that we had purchased, and dealers began lining up, waiting for us to call their areas. Who knows how far we would have gone with that, but it had a short life. As I said, we had a love/hate relationship, and it was coming to a head.

The basic problem was that the Circulation Department at The News wanted the best of both worlds. They treated and expected the franchise dealers to behave as employees. However, they wanted no part of the employee benefits that went along with an employer/employee relationship. The union agreements were already sucking them dry, and they didn't want to add to the problem. So, contracts were signed to confirm that the dealers were independent businessmen, and responsible for any losses that they might incur in the operation of such business. Then they proceeded to prod the dealers to make bad business decisions, just so long as they achieved the short-term goal of increasing circulation. Their behavior was understandable, because advertising rates were directly proportional to circulation, and home delivered circulation was at a premium.

From day one, we complied with everything that made good business sense, and resisted all others. They may not have liked it, but they couldn't argue with success. They liked us even less when we formed the Franchise Dealers Association. This became a forum for the Suffolk dealers, who as a result became more informed and more resistant to pressure. As officers of the association, Mike and I reached out to groups of dealers in Nassau County and Brooklyn. The News always interpreted the associations as anti-News, but it wasn't necessarily so. The goal was to have a better business relationship with The News, but they preferred to go the dictatorial route. Unfortunate circumstances brought everything to a head!

## The ultimatum

The News in Co-op City, like Long Island, was being delivered by carrier boys. Unlike Long Island, this was not residential. All deliveries were being made in thirty-story buildings. After a time, there occurred incidences where the boys were being mugged in the stairwells on the days that they were collecting money for their deliveries. We alerted security, advised carriers not to go around alone, and to vary the time that they went out to collect. It didn't get any better, and as word spread, boys became fearful, and our delivery system became strained to the point that we had to make a decision. So, when we were unable to replace a carrier boy, deliveries were turned over to an adult carrier, and we paid him for the deliveries made. When a carrier was found, he would collect for those days, and keep the extra tips. Unfortunately, we lost more carriers than we gained. So, we started billing subscribers directly, by the month. At least half the carrier profit was dependent on tips, which were lost when billing. Without the tips, we couldn't afford to pay the men. So, we adjusted the subscriber rate to include the equivalent of a modest tip. Then gradually, as the need arose, we converted to an adult delivery system. The increased price and adult delivery were direct violations of our contract, but we had no other choice!

When Mike was summoned to a meeting at The News Building in Manhattan, we assumed that they had found out what we were doing, and were going to give us a hard time. He was ready with facts and figures, and left for the morning meeting. When he came back to our Bay Shore office in the late afternoon, his face was ashen!

He said that he had been escorted into the office of the Circulation Director, who was accompanied by three other regional managers, and asked to sit in a chair in front of the desk. He was then told that his contract was being terminated immediately, and that he no longer had a business in Co-op City! That was the only reason he had been asked to come in, and the meeting was over! Mike's mind had gone numb. He had not been prepared for anything like this. Through the confusion, he desperately tried to think of what to do, because they were getting up to leave. As I listened to his story for the first time, I imagined myself sitting in that chair, and felt the same sensations that he had felt!

Mike said that the only thing that he could think of was that he had to stop them from leaving. He didn't remember what he had said, but they stopped to hear him out. As his brain cleared a little, he was able to get them to sit down again, and to reconsider their actions. The rest of the day was spent on how fast he was going to get back into the fold. He had agreed to a period of thirty days. Hours later, without panic, and with a cool head, it was almost impossible to believe that they had actually planned to go ahead with their plan. To cut off thousands in circulation didn't make sense, and these people also had to answer to others above them for their actions. Maybe, but you never know! Thank God, we didn't have to find out.

## The biggest gamble of our lives

*I'm going to be rather detailed in describing our challenge to The News, both because it was a major event in our lives, and because it had both intense and entertaining moments. If courtroom drama and intrigue bores you, then know that we sued The News, and move forward to the heading, "My personal life in the 60's."*

We talked over our options. Converting back to the old system in Co-op City was not practical. If it had been, we never would have changed over in the first place. Selling was another option. However, the new owner would face the same problems that we had, and unless we got an all-cash deal, we would also lose money. I suppose that other options became less attractive because, as we talked, we became angrier and angrier at the way we had been treated! Nobody should have the right to do what they had just done! So, we met with our trusty attorney Ted Daniels, to explore any legal options. He took our contract home to read, and told us to come back the next day. When we did, he told us that it was a good contract, and The News was within its rights. He said that he had also asked his wife what she thought, and she had concurred with his assessment. It was then that we realized that either Ted didn't know what he was talking about, or that our thinking was way off base. Since we were firm in our beliefs, we decided to look further.

We consulted with an older attorney that had also done some dealings for us. He was close to retirement, was very thorough, and had been considered for a judgeship. After listening to us, he agreed that we had a case, but not by challenging the contract directly. We had to sue The News on anti-trust violations, and we needed big-name attorneys to take them on. He then took down a book that detailed the law firms in Manhattan, and whittled it down to the best three anti-trust firms there.

You know the old saying, "I'd rather be lucky than good?" Well, that's how we met Nick Coch. The first two firms that we called, the secretaries took a message, and told us that someone would get back to us. The third, White and Coch, was answered by Nick Coch himself. He listened to our story, wanted to hear more, and advised that time was of the essence. He suggested that we meet the next day, at a diner on Long Island, which was halfway between us. We later found out that White and Coch was an attorney's attorney, doing work for other firms, and highly regarded in the field. That's why the phone had been answered directly. Nick originally thought that we had called him by mistake, meaning to call the larger and more prestigious firm, "Coch and White."

After listening to what we had to say, Nick thought that we had a very good case. However, if we were going to take on The News, we had to realize that it was going to take a few years, and would be very expensive. Although he liked the case very much, his was a small firm, and didn't have deep financial pockets. They couldn't afford a full contingency, but he would talk to his partners, and see what he could do. We were very impressed with him, both as a person, and as an attorney. As we would find out was his way, he got back to us promptly. His partners also liked the case, and the opportunity to take on Goliath. So, they agreed to take a small monthly contingency fee, but we would have to pay for any ongoing expenses. It seemed like something that we could afford, and we agreed. In fact, Nick had just become our business partner!

Mike's meeting in the city quickly spread to the lower help, I imagine accompanied by stories of how those pain-in-the-ass Lepore brothers had finally been brought to heel! How else to explain the smirks on the faces of the reps at the next weekly meeting, and how more authoritative their tone had become. Even our fellow dealers began to distance themselves from us, with the exception of Arnie Blume. In fact, both Mike and I were summoned into the city, where we were told in no uncertain terms, how we were going to operate our business from then on. Tony Catanzaro, the regional circulation manager, wagged his finger across the table at us, and warned, "If you don't do exactly as I say, I'm going to make it my job to drum you out of the business, and make sure you never get back in." John White, his assistant, kept nodding for emphasis. This infuriated me to the point that I stood up, walked towards the door, and challenged John to step out in the hallway with me. The piss-ass wouldn't move, and calmer minds settled me down, but I will never forget that day!

I remember the day The News found out that we were not the sheep that they thought we were. In preparing for our case, Nick contacted the attorney for the Independent Dealers Association in the city. They had a class case going on with The News, and Nick decided it would be a good idea to testify on behalf of the dealers. So, Mike was called to testify in Federal Court in Manhattan. When we walked into the courtroom, we saw Tony Catanzaro, John White, Jack Underwood, and some local reps. Upon first seeing us, they thought that we had come to support them, and broke out in big grins from ear to ear. When we didn't smile back, and passed them, with Nick carrying folders of papers, the smiles faded, and we heard, "Oh shit!"

It didn't take long for retribution to start. Almost immediately, they terminated our telephone business. We had no contract, and no recourse. Then, they started sending reps down to Co-op City at night, following and questioning our delivery people. Our people had full time jobs, and were delivering newspapers to earn a few extra dollars. They didn't want any drama, and some wanted to quit. Nick said that the only way to make them stop was to get an injunction against them. He filed the papers, but told us it was a very long shot; reason being that in granting an injunction, the judge was giving you right before going to trial. So, he had to be really convinced that you were being irreparably harmed. Plus, damages in an antitrust case are tripled, so that we would be more than compensated if we won the case. The fact was that if we had no business, we had no income, and couldn't go forward with the case. So, we had no choice but to try.

## The showdown at the OK corral

The day of the hearing, we went to Federal Court in lower Manhattan in high anxiety. Due to The News' pressure, other dealers avoided us like the plague, and that included even our "closest" friends. There was one exception. Nick Carulli was a small dealer from Eastern Suffolk, who was having his own troubles with The News, but chose to come in with us, and testify on our behalf. It was a very courageous thing for him to do. When we took our places, the disparity was ridiculous. The Daily News' legal office occupied a whole floor in The Daily News building, and their representatives showed up in force, headed by the chief of the firm Andy Hughes. The suits filed in, and additional chairs were needed to accommodate the overflow of attorneys around their table. On our side, we could have fit comfortably around a card table! It was clear that they intended to steamroll us with the power of The Daily News. Certainly, they scared the Hell out of me!

Nick Coch is about 5'5", bespectacled, very soft-spoken, and with an average build. His appearance doesn't strike fear into anyone's heart, but he was supremely confident in his abilities, and wasn't frightened by bluster. He had taken on the government for a few years in the famous milk wars of New Jersey, and come out a winner. So, we started calling witnesses, and proceeded with the hearing. For Mike and me, it was like being in an emotional elevator. When Nick had finished his questioning, we knew we had a great case, and winning was in the bag. Then, when opposing counsels had finished their cross-examination, we realized that we had embarked on a lost cause. Up and down, up and down, until recess. After lunch, Nick's partner Stewart joined us. Stu was always traveling, fighting for environmental causes. We were told that he was brilliant, and came from "old money". Where Nick was strong in writing legal briefs, Stu's specialty was interrogation and presentation. He explained that his job was "to turn the light bulb on in the judge's head." The judge would then look at the submitted briefs the way that we wanted him to. In our case, it was to make him see that this had nothing to do with the contract, and was indeed an antitrust case.

When we resumed the hearing, Stu took over and called Carlton Rosenberg to the stand. Rosenberg was the chief financial officer at The Daily News, and had been involved from the beginning with the Franchise Delivery Program. We knew where Stu was going, but the other side didn't. It was exciting to watch and listen. He appeared to ask perfectly innocent questions, and Carlton had no clue that he was being set up. It was like watching a surgeon operating with words, slicing away until he got to where he wanted. He reviewed the founding of the Co-op City franchise, how it had been different from all other operations, how the art department had produced special promotions only for Co-op City, how the franchise had been a first in many ways, and how successful we had been at it. This had been going on for a while, and was actually becoming boring to judge Gurfein, who appeared to be listening with his eyes closed. What followed was memorable! Stu asked, "So, Mr. Rosenberg, based on what you've been telling me, would it be fair to say that so far as the Co-op City franchise operation and the relationship with Mr. Lepore is concerned, you were sailing in unchartered waters?" Without waiting for the answer, he turned to face us, stuck his thumbs in his vest pockets, and gave us a big wink! Looking over his shoulder, we saw the judge's eyes swing open, sit up in his chair, and wait for the answer, which was "Yes." Honest-to-God, we could almost see a physical light bulb come on above the judge's head! The chief counsel for The News then took over for the cross-examination. He immediately started asking questions that related to our violations of the contracted agreement. After the first two or three, the judge interrupted him to ask, "Excuse me Mr. Hughes, but haven't you been listening to what's been going on here? This isn't a contractual thing; it's an antitrust thing! I strongly suggest that you reconvene in your offices, and map out a new strategy. I've heard enough." The attorneys looked at one another, and didn't know what to say. They had been totally surprised by the tactic. However, they were all very embarrassed, and looked it. It was priceless! We walked out on cloud nine, and in a week's time, we had our Injunction. The News had to supply us with the newspapers that we requested to service Co-op City, and not to engage in any tactics that could be construed as harassment.

Having secured Co-op City, we felt that they would try to get even with us on Long Island. In fact, they tried to intimidate dealers from associating with us, and harassing some who did. One dealer, Larry Hodas, was funny. He came to us and said, "Look, I like you guys, and I'm with you, but I'm just a little Jewish guy. I'm not a fighter, and these guys are following me around at night, harassing me, and copying down the addresses that I'm delivering to. Sooner or later, they're going to dump me." So, we hired a bodyguard with a gun to ride around with him for a couple of weeks, in which time his local attorney filed a claim against The News, and the harassment stopped.

Nick agreed to seek a second injunction for Long Island, but this time they were ready, and the odds against us were even greater than the first time. The News knew that they had to defend against an antitrust challenge, and would adjust accordingly. Plus, we had not been harmed or harassed there, with the exception of the loss of the phone room. Also, the Bay Shore/Brentwood franchise was not as unique as Co-op City. We hoped to hang our hat on the fact that Mike and I were joined at the hip, and were seen as such by The News. So, if one was in danger, so was the other.

Once again, we went to the Federal Court Building in lower Manhattan. This time, The News was not represented by an avalanche of attorneys. They weren't trying to win just on reputation, but they were represented by the chief counsel of the firm, Andy Hughes. This time, I wasn't as intimidated. As we waited for our turn to appear before a very busy judge, I was fascinated by the case that was being argued before us. This was a big case, being argued by top attorneys, in front of a very sharp judge, and I was drawn into it. However, since I wasn't emotionally involved, I wasn't riding that elevator up and down, as I had at our first hearing. Rather, it was like watching a verbal tennis match as my attention shifted from one side to another. After one side had made its presentation, I would think, "Oh that's good." Then the other side would have its say, and I would think, "Oh that's better." Then the judge would pick apart both presentations, ask some questions that both attorneys had trouble answering, and I would think, "Wow, how did he pick up on those things?" It was all very exhilarating. I've liked lawyer shows ever since.

Finally, our turn came. Stu was not around this time, so Nick presented our case, as did The News' counsel. No witnesses were called. Judge Duffy then took us all into his chambers and asked us to sit. He explained how very busy he was, but that he understood the case, and asked for time to properly respond. He asked both sides to give him thirty days and not to do anything that would change the status quo for that period. Both sides agreed, and we left. Other than getting a thirty-day protection order, we had no idea how the judge might rule. Fortunately for us, The News' vaunted legal team came to our rescue.

They weren't sure how the judge was going to rule either, and didn't want to take a chance on an adverse ruling. So, they interpreted the judge's request to mean just not to harass us, and do an end run around our challenge. This would be to take us out of Federal Court, and bring us into State Court on a straight contract violation suit. Once filed, that case would take precedence over our antitrust case! Nick was served with the papers of intent, and he petitioned the federal judge for an immediate emergency meeting. When we all showed up in court this time, only the attorneys were asked back into the judge's chambers. They weren't gone very long. When they came out, it was easy to tell the winner from the losers. Nick was all smiles, while the troop of the other attorneys had that hangdog look of kids who had just lost all their marbles. Nick told us that in his professional life, he had never seen anything like it. Judge Duffy had asked for confirmation of what The News' attorneys were planning to do. They confirmed. Then he asked them if they remembered to have agreed to give him thirty days. They remembered. They never got to say another word! The judge spent the rest of the time tearing into them for their unprofessional conduct. Now, these were senior attorneys of a very prestigious law firm, and they were being dressed down in no uncertain terms, in front of Nick, from a younger attorney, who happened to be the judge. Nick said that if he hadn't been enjoying it so much, he would have been embarrassed! The payoff was that we were granted an immediate Injunction on all counts, and The News' attorneys were warned to honor the letter of the law. Then they were told to get out! Once again, we had beaten great odds.

So, we were doing well in business, and having that business protected until the resolution of the case. Then, there was the possibility of a huge win, but that was too far away, with no guarantee of success. The salvage of our business had been the goal, and we had achieved it.

## My personal life in the 60's

It may seem that the only important thing in my life during this period was the business or business-connected, and that I had no personal life. Nothing could be further from the truth! While true that everything personal flowed from the income that was generated from our activities; we did not live to work! We worked so as to have a better life, and more fun!

So it was that we were able to vacation frequently at Lake George with Mike and Pat, spend a year in Italy with Mario and Nancy, and other getaways during the decade.

Marco was a beautiful boy, joined by Gregory in "61, and Marisa in "66. We made for a good-looking family, even if I do say so myself. In the same period, Mario and Nancy had Donna, Michele, and Elisa. Mike and Pat had Maria and Michael. So, we had grown to a rather large family. So much so, that it became hard to have an all get-together, although I do remember one such holiday at Mike's house in Kings Park. Generally, Pat's parents would drive out from the Bronx, and bring my father and Enza with them. We'd eat and then play poker at Mike's place. Also, Nancy's mother and sister's family would come, and we would eat and party with them, mostly at Mario's house. We would also host parties at our place. In the early part of the decade, before we had our homes, the get-togethers would be by us in Franklin Square, or by the Termines in the Bronx. Of course, there were the frequent visits to my father and Enza, as well as getting together with Mike and Pat at their apartment in Freeport.

We seemed to have two lives. One was with Mario and Nancy, and one was with Mike and Pat, and occasionally all together. All the lives were great, and they were great years!

What made it special for Aida and I was that, from the very beginning, we shared living quarters and lives with Mario and Nancy. Together in Franklin Square for almost ten years, and then in adjoining homes in St. James thereafter, we shared and enjoyed our growing pains. Along the way, we matched kid for kid. They got on the board quickly with Donna, and Marco had a buddy. Greg was matched nine months later with Michele, and they became buddies. They came up with Elisa, and we caught up five months later with Marisa. Aida and Nancy were best buddies, as were

Mario and I. Strangely, even though Mario and I almost never agreed on anything, we still had a lot of fun together.

Sometimes, we did foolish things. I've already told about buying the Kirby vacuum cleaners. Another was the time we thought we could afford a couple of days vacation, but didn't want to waste our money. So, Mario and I left at midnight to drive to the Catskills, about four hours away, so that we could check out the rooms at the Shawanga Lodge. The people there thought we were nuts.

My in-laws visited occasionally from Italy, and we looked forward to their coming. On one of these trips, my mother-in-law decided that she was going to straighten out our marriages. She was very sincere, and it wasn't until Nancy and I compared notes that we saw the humor in it.

One day, while Mario was at work, she sat down with Nancy, and gave her some marital advice. "Nancy, you need to be more understanding. You spend the day here at home, nice and sheltered in this house, without anybody bothering you. Mario instead is out there in the world, trying to earn a living. He has to put up with a lot stuff and people. So, when he comes home, he needs to relax and unwind. It's up to you to make his life at home as pleasant as possible." Nancy appreciated the advice and agreed to do her best.

The same day, after I got home from work, she took me aside for my marital advice. "Vito, you need to be more understanding. You spend the day out of the house, meeting people and having a good time. Aida instead is stuck here in the house with the baby, cooking and cleaning. So, when you come home, you need to help her relax and unwind. It's up to you to make her life at home as pleasant as possible." I also agreed.

When we played back to her what she had said to us, she still didn't see anything wrong with it. As I said, she was very sincere.

Mario was going through his own growing pains, and I think it was harder for him because he was doing it alone, while I had my brother. It was true that he saw himself as the heir to the pastificio, but that was in the future, and he had the present to contend with. It was complicated by the fact that his mother would occasionally ask for his help in Italy, and he would drop everything and go. If his business had been thriving, it might have been a different story.

The car wash started going bad, and he got out of it. He went to work for Grunman for a few months before we went to Italy in 1963, and he went to work in the pastificio. When they came back in 1965, he invested in a donut shop in Manhattan, and commuted daily, putting in long hours. It was doing well until Choc ful o'nuts opened a few blocks away, and he was forced to sell. Back to Italy again, but with three children, it wasn't a solution. They didn't want the kids to grow up in Italy, and possibly get stuck there.

Back home, this time joining us next door in St. James, he invested in a vinyl top business. This consisted of putting vinyl tops and/or body side-moldings on cars, and provided him with his income for many years. Without him at the pastificio, the brothers were able to pressure the sister into selling her share to them, which also closed the door for Mario. Of course it's a lot more complicated than I've explained, but that's the general picture.

\* \* \*

## Enjoying the children

Having four, and then five years between children was great for me. There was always a little one around, and I enjoyed taking them on vacation as much as I enjoyed the vacation itself. I looked forward to the ceremony of putting them to bed at night, after Aida had bathed and powdered them up. They each had their own style. Marco wanted a Superman ride, but he had to earn it. He had to be very serious as he came in from the other room, stop and say, "This is a job for Superman!" Then, he would bound up, with arms outstretched, and say, "Up, up, and awayyy". I would catch him on his way up, and make sure that he flew all the way to his bed. If he smirked or didn't do it seriously, he would have to do it all over again.

Greg wanted either an elephant ride or an airplane ride. The elephant ride consisted of me bending forward, dropping my arms, and interlocking my fingers. This made it an elephant's trunk, and I started to waddle, making the proper elephant noise. Then, Greg would sit in my trunk, and instantly become Tarzan. The elephant wouldn't move unless given the proper instructions, which was the order, "Ungauaa". Of course, if he didn't say, "Ungauaa" again to stop, I would go running into walls and tables and such. Directions had to be given. It sometimes took a while to make it to the bedroom. The airplane ride consisted of him getting on my back, while I made airplane motor sounds with outstretched arms. He had to push forward on the ears, or pull on them for directions. We always wound up with a crazy airplane, and it also took a while to get to the bedroom.

When Marisa came around, it was a two-parter. First, she wanted to be launched as a rocket unto her bed. So, we would have a rocket-launch-countdown, and then she would free-fly unto the bed. As she became used to it, the launch was backed up, and the toss was higher, and she enjoyed seeing how high she bounced off the mattress. Then, settled in bed, I would read her a story from her book collection. Eventually, it turned out to be the same one every night, "Sleeping Beauty". However, she had to pay attention, because whenever I would stop reading, she had to say what was coming next, and say it with the proper conviction. My favorite stops were the arrival of Malificent, the names of the fairy godmothers, and the order, "Let all the spindles and spinning wheels be <u>burnt!</u>" She said this last with great conviction.

Greg was five years older, but he listened in from the bedroom next door, and complained when I didn't read loud enough. He also had another request for me. Invariably, when I left for work around 3:00 AM, he was awake, and would ask for a glass of water. I would then have to fill a glass of water, drape a towel over my raised left arm, go stand by his bed, and in my best imitation of an English butler, say, "You called, sir?" Even if he wasn't thirsty, he had to drink the whole glass. After which, I would take the glass with a "Thank you, sir!" He would giggle, and I'd go on my business.

Eventually, I started making up my own stories, which were a variation of different fables, and they came to know "Aladdin and the Mina-Mina bird." The Mina-Mina bird had the head of a dragon, the wings of an eagle, the body of a lion, and a whip for a tail. He also could breathe fire. Unfortunately, he also had big floppy feet that wouldn't go how he wanted them to, and he wasn't too bright. Oh, and he also breathed fire on people after an accidental hiccup. He was lovable, but got into a lot of trouble. Aladdin had his magic lamp and the Genie, but the Genie didn't like the Mina-Mina bird. There was the villain Fu-man-chu, a very short villain with a very long Fu-man-chu mustache, who was always scheming to steal Aladdin's lamp. It wasn't hard to make up stories.

When Marco was about eleven, I took them all on. First, I would sit on the floor, cross-legged like a Buddha, and challenged Marco and Greg to knock me over. They would start running from the other side of the den, and with great determination barrel into me. When I didn't go down, it was usually Greg's fault, according to Marco. After about a year, they got me down.

All three of them liked when I was "The sleeping monster". The Cyclops monster was asleep in the den, but he was going to wake up soon. They had to hold him so that he couldn't move when he did wake up. Marco of course directed his brother and sister on what to hold, but the chore was made more difficult because the monster was tossing in his sleep. Eventually, the monster would awaken, and with a loud, "Ahh, I smell the blood of an Englishman!" would break all the holds, and bite them while they screamed.

There was more, and I enjoyed it as much as they did. They were priceless years, and no matter how old they get, I always remember them as little ones.

\* \* \*

In the adult world, the roller-coaster ride of the business world was not brought home. I didn't share my anxieties with Aida in Italy, or any others in the ensuing years. Of course, when things were tough, it was self-evident, as it was when things were going well, but so long as she didn't feel confusion or overwhelmed, it was fine. She and Mario had grown up in that atmosphere, and had never gotten over it. It helped that she wasn't inquisitive about the details of our business. Her focus was to keep her domain clean and orderly, and that was whether it was the villino in Trani, the basement, the dormer, or the big house in St. James. When the kids came along, the clean and orderly tag applied to them as well. In time, this came to work against her, because she wouldn't delegate any of the chores. No one could do them as well, so as the family and the house grew, the chores became just a lot of daily work. Fortunately, with Nancy near, there was always a reason for a coffee break.

I've already noted how important it was for me not to worry about shelter during this period, thanks to my in-laws. However, when the time came that I was ready to go out on my own, they again were a big help.

In the late 60's, although we were recovering financially, we were not putting much money away. Everything was invested. So, when we started house-hunting, I found myself in a strange predicament; I could afford to carry the expenses of the big houses that we were looking at, but I didn't have the cash required for the down payment. Then, when I did have the cash and went back, the price had gone up, as well as the down payment. It seemed to be a losing spiral.

Fortunately, or unfortunately, this also was the time when Mario and Nancy decided that they didn't want to raise their family in Italy. Mario found two adjoining properties in an exclusive development in St. James, in the township of Smithtown. Still, I didn't have enough for the down payment. My in-laws came to the rescue. They bought Mario's house for him as reward for his dedication to them. They also gave us the difference for what we needed to make the down payment, so that we could continue to live together. All that was left to do was for Mario and me to go unto our properties and pee on them so as to take full possession. Again, thank you mom and dad.

The beginning at the house has a couple of funny stories. We didn't have enough furniture for the four bedrooms, two-and-a-half baths, a full parlor, dining room, and den. Having visions of grandeur, I thought I should hire an interior decorator. Our accountant recommended one that was highly regarded. He came out to visit, took notes, and then we met him in Manhattan. We visited various showrooms open only to decorators and such, taking cabs from one to the next. Aida wasn't impressed with any of them. The reason was that the items were stored with a lot of other items, and it required imagination to see how they would look in our house. The decorator had it, but we didn't, and we weren't going to put anything in our house that we didn't like. After a few hours, we decided to break for lunch. As we settled into our seats at the restaurant, Aida commented, "Now isn't this nice? Comfortable chairs, nice wide table, and lots of leg room. Why can't we find something like this for us?" The decorator finally realized that we had no artistic soul at all, and were a lost cause. His face lit up, "I have your solution! I've been bringing you to the wrong places. We're going to go where they show the furnishings for motels and restaurants! Maybe you will find a check-out counter that you would like for your kitchen." He was obviously thoroughly disgusted with us, but when he brought us to that showroom; it was just what we wanted. I designed the kitchen table and chairs that I wanted, and have enjoyed the set to this very day.

Having lost our guide, we were on our own. We found a bedroom set that we liked, and the store manager proceeded to tell us what a great choice we had made. Thomasville was a top of the line product, and our satisfaction was guaranteed. We were assured that after the set had been delivered and assembled, they would send a man over to double-check and fix any nicks or scratches that might be on the furniture. Sure enough, after the delivery, Aida called the store. She told the manager, "OK, the bed is all assembled, and I'm ready for the man. When will he here?" Telling me the story, she was puzzled as to why there was silence on the line for a couple of minutes.

Of course, I passed the story on, and everybody got a kick out of it. A few evenings later, the doorbell rang. There stood our neighbor, Jack Kalabza, in a full-length red flannel nightgown, complete with stocking cap, holding a can of furniture polish. With a very serious face he said, "Please tell Mrs. Lepore that the man is here."

Of course there were some bumps, but life was overwhelmingly positive at 29 Glenrich Drive.

*   *   *

**Back to the war...**

The two injunctions protected our business, which in turn financed our lawsuit. It was made clear that it might take a few years for a resolution, and we just couldn't sit on our hands until the time came to go to court. We had to gather evidence and prepare for that day. As a first step, Nick Coch filed a motion for discovery, wanting to see some records that The News had relevant to its franchise business, and asked that they be brought to court before the judge.

I've since seen this move done a few times in lawyer movies, when a large and prestigious firm wants to steamroll a smalltime lawyer. Rather than show up with a few folders, they came in force with boxes and boxes of papers for us to inspect. The judge was sympathetic, but would allow us only a couple of hours to view the contents. He recessed the hearing for that long.

Nick was unperturbed. He had come prepared for dirty tricks. He suggested we go out for lunch, while his young assistant looked over the files. That young assistant had a portable tape recorder, and all he did for the next two hours was read out folder names, and some sheet headings from each folder. In that manner, he was able to go through almost all the boxes in the two hours. When we reconvened, Nick advised the judge that he would be requesting copies of specific documents and contents of named folders. The judge agreed, and advised The News to deliver all that was requested. The News didn't know to what extent we had identified the contents, and they didn't want to be in contempt again. They complied fully.

So it was that we found ourselves with a treasure trove of inside information, including internal memos and so much more than we had hoped for. Once again, David had slammed Goliath.

Maybe because Nick was so unassuming, it took The News a little while to realize that it was in serious trouble. That day may have come when we were summoned to The News building, and took the elevator up to the rarified top floors, where only the biggest chiefs roam. We were escorted into the office of Jack Underwood, who was the architect of the franchise system.

We were properly intimidated, and Mr. Underwood began to berate us for how thankless we were. Nick listened for a bit, then interrupted, "Excuse me, but you don't talk to them. You talk to me. I'm the hired gun, and I'm here to tell you that you can no longer do what you've been doing. If you want to talk settlement, fine. Otherwise, we'll see you in court." With that, we got up and left. We felt so much taller.

## Strategies, strategies, strategies:

There appeared to always be a reason to confer with Nick, and we would meet at his office in Manhattan. About this time, his fortunes had also dramatically risen. He had taken a position offered by a prestigious law firm, Anderson, Russell, Kill, and Olick. It had a whole floor in the building overlooking the skating rink in Rockefeller Center, and Nick had a bunch of lawyers working for him. Now he had more guns with which to go after The News. It was pretty heady stuff for us. Heady and expensive! When we would break for lunch or stay for dinner; we would go to the gallery below the building, or around the corner to Charley O's, and once to the Rainbow room. It was there that I ordered my first "quick" Lorraine. I had never heard or seen the word "quiche". Fortunately, they all thought I was kidding (except Mike).

Once again, it became necessary to divide our responsibilities. The legal stuff required a lot of time, but we still had a business to run. Mike was the point man in the revolution, so his presence was requested more and more. I was happy to stay back; too much strategizing gave me a headache. So it was that Mike and Nick became best buddies. They fed off each other, and we all benefitted. In gathering evidence, they travelled to California to confer with attorneys that were challenging the publishers there; they went to D.C. to confer with senators, and Mike even testified before one of their committees; they went out-of-state to interview possible witnesses. Nick came to appreciate Mike's input, and they made a great team.

This was in the early 70's, and I want to note how far Mike had come from the kid of 1960. As I've said many times, he was always intelligent, insightful, and determined, but he was eight years behind me. I had the best seat in the house as I watched him mature, and really come into his own in the period of the law suit. I attended a session where he was being questioned during a deposition by a battery of attorneys for The News. Clearly, they were trying to trip him up, and had it been me, they would have been successful. He was able to deliberate quickly, while I was still trying to figure it out on the ride back home. Moreover, he kept the lines of communication open, and that turned out to be crucial.

Not all the schemes were good; one was particularly ill-advised. Nick had not been successful in getting a Teamster union boss to come in for a deposition. Reviewing this at a bar after a meeting, we all became properly pissed-off. So, we promptly returned to Nick's office, where he drafted a subpoena for the union leader, found out his home address, and called in one of his young attorneys to go serve it. To be sure that it go well, he suggested that Mike and I go along to serve as witnesses. We willingly agreed.

We went in the young attorney's car out to the union boss's house in Brooklyn. There, we were told that he was not expected home until late. Rather than accept defeat, we decided to stake out the house. The kid was clearly nervous, our drinks had worn off, and we were about to give up at 1:00AM. Suddenly, a car comes and pulls into the garage under the house, the door opening electronically. We were shocked into action! We realized that if we didn't move quickly, the garage door would close, and we would lose our opportunity. As one, we jumped out of our car, and went rushing into the garage, just as a big burly guy had gotten out of his car. You can imagine his reaction at seeing three people rushing at him in the middle of the night!

I think what may have saved us was his total surprise, and that the young attorney was waving the subpoena in the air, shouting that he was there to serve it. When finally able to speak, he was furious, and his language isn't printable. Cleaned up, it was something like, "How stupid are you guys? I could have blown you away, and then gone upstairs and had a good night's sleep." He took the subpoena, and we drove home in silence, contemplating what could have been.

\* \* \*

We kept the dealers updated through our Association and that of the Brooklyn dealers. Nick attended a general session, and detailed what their rights were. He was confident that we had a very good antitrust case, and had a couple of recent Supreme Court decisions that were in our favor; The Schwinn bicycle case, and the Coor's beer case.

The News found itself in a bind. It couldn't make long-term plans because it didn't know how the case was going to turn out, and didn't know how to handle the static it was getting from the dealers in the meantime. It also must have been aware that they might lose, paying triple damages. That would explain the beginning of a shift in personnel, and the sudden respect shown us. As I've explained, Mike (the velvet glove) had kept the lines of communication open, and he began to be approached by lower level managers about his opinion on things. It was clear that they were messengers, and he kept moving up the food chain, until he got to meet the new top dog, Jim Artz. This guy was as personable as the others had been offensive. I went in with Mike for a lunch meeting one day, and the two of them were like frat brothers. I felt like the odd-man-out.

It went on like that for a few months. Jim Artz would say that he didn't want to bring the attorneys in until a deal was hammered out, as if everything that he said hadn't been previously cleared by them. Likewise, Mike couldn't get on the phone with Nick fast enough after each session, to review and agree on the marching orders for the next time. Mike did a great job. It's fair to say that a settlement would not have happened without him. Even more important, we found out a few years later that the legal winds had shifted a bit against us, had we gone to court.

We knew we were close to an agreement the day we got a call telling us that Jim Artz was coming out to Long Island,

and taking us out to dinner at a restaurant near our office. It was a momentous day, but for me it was monumental! When he arrived, we saw that he had been chauffeured out by Tony Catanzaro. Yes, the Tony Catanzaro that a couple of years before had wagged his finger under our noses, and told us he was going to drive us out of the business!

Whether by order or not, he did not socialize with us as he drove to the restaurant. At the restaurant, he was told to wait at the bar while we went in for dinner, in case there may have been a question for him. The dinner was long and full of sugar plums; we were getting a confirmation of what had already been worked out. I don't think my feet hit the floor as we made our way out and picked up Tony, who was sitting at the bar nursing a drink with a most dejected lonely look on his face. For me, that was the cherry on the sundae!

## The aftershock

After that, everything moved quickly, but you couldn't prove it by us. We knew that nothing had been signed yet, and it could blow up at any minute. That's what attorneys do. Even when we went in to sign, we weren't sure they would pay. The News also had to get it past some of their people, so they hid some of the payout money in the form of no-show consulting contracts for Mike and me. Also, they wanted a clean slate, so we arranged for a 20K payment to the Jewish dealer who had filed against them. When we called him with the news, he thought he had hit the lottery.

Finally, payment was made to Nick's law firm, and the check cleared. We went to his office to pick up our share, after his 30%. We figured Nick's check would be good.

On the personal vendetta side; Tony Catanzaro wound up leaving, and getting a low-level manager job at Newsday; John White (the guy who wouldn't come out in the hallway with me) was fired, and also wound up being a low-level rep at Newsday; Jack Underwood (the big banana) was fired or resigned. We were told he had wound up in California, running a car wash (maybe he bought it). Life was sweet.

On the business side, The News rewrote all the franchise contracts, giving more independence to the dealers; such as removing price, territorial restrictions, or methods of delivery. It would be poetic to say that the dealers learned something, but it wouldn't be true. However, that's another story, and beyond the scope of this book.

## Mike moves to Florida

Since the early 70's, Mike and Pat had expressed a desire to move out of New York. They were attracted to Florida, and began exploring the area. They started on the east coast, vacationing from Miami on up to Vero Beach, but were not satisfied. Recommended to the Gulf Coast, they found Sarasota and loved it. They didn't move there right away, but told everyone what a great place it was. So it was that their best friends Tommy Rumpf and Barbara went to see for themselves, and immediately moved there. Then, Pat's sister Barbara had just married Bob Lombardo, and they went to take a look. They both got jobs there and immediately relocated. When Mike and Pat finally decided to make their move permanent, it was almost like going home.

## Tying up loose ends

We had been at it with The News for five years when we finally settled in 1977. As a condition, they also wanted us out of Co-Op City. They agreed to approve and help finance a new buyer. Mike came up with a guy who was part of a poker club, had cash, and was looking for an investment. Boy, did we have deal for him! He was also a diamond merchant with an office just around from Rockefeller Center. That deal turned out to be as funny as it was profitable.

The long and short of it was that we now had an embarrassment of riches, and no plan as to what to do. We had made a financial quantum leap, didn't know what the future held, but had visions of sugar plums.

The general plan was for Mike to start up some new business in Florida, with me investing some money in the ventures. If successful, we would reunite some time in the future. In the meantime, I would run the operation on Long Island, and send Mike payments for his share of the business. Truthfully, the monies paled in comparison to the settlement.

Mike had been commuting between Florida and New York for the last few years, but when his final move came, it was still a big jolt for me. We had travelled a long road together, and it was much more than just the business. Our sense of humor was not understood by everybody, and we knew we were in a class all by ourselves. We had made a great team, and besides losing my brother, I was losing my best buddy. Also, who was I going to play handball with now? It wasn't fun with anybody else.

# EPILOGUE

That's the end of this book, but there's more. After all, in 1977 I'm only 47, Mike is 39, and we have money. What does the future hold? Mmmmmmmmm!

What I've hoped to have shown is that the road of life is a never-ending series of crossroads, some by accident, and some by design. Your life can change on any given day. It then follows that there is no such thing as a last chance, and that failure is part of the learning process. What's required is that a person be involved and commit.

Happy trails,

Vito